How Old Is Your Church?

An Introductory Guide to Catholic Apologetics

KEN LITCHFIELD

ISBN-13: 9781790982691

DEDICATION

This book is dedicated to my wife Debbie and all of my Catholic and Protestant friends that inspired me to help explain the Catholic Faith.

ACKNOWLEDGMENT

I want to thank the many Catholic and Protestant apologists that I have from so that I could write this book. You will find most of them listed in the additional resources at the end of this book.

Table of Contents

Churches and Their Founders

Church	Founder	Year
Catholic Church	Jesus	33 AD
Orthodox Church	Jesus	33 AD
Lutheran	Martin Luther	1517
Swiss Reformed	Ulrich Zwingli	1523
Mennonites	Grebel, Mantz & Blaurock	1525
Anglican	Henry the VIII	1534
Calvinism	John Calvin	1536
Presbyterian	John Knox	1560
Baptist	John Smyth	1605
Quakers	George Fox	1647
Amish	Jacob Ammann	1693
Methodist	John + Charles Wesley	1739
Congregational	Robert Brown	1744
Episcopalian	Samuel Seabury	1789
United Brethren	Otterbein & Boehm	1800
Church of Christ	Tom & Alex Campbell	1829
Mormons	Joseph Smith	1830
Seventh Day Adventists	William Miller	1860
Salvation Army	William Booth	1865
Jehovah Witness	Charles Taze Russel	1874
Christian Science	Mary Baker Eddy	1879
Pentecostal	Charles Parham	1900
Four Square Gospel	Aimee McPherson	1917
Assembly of God	Assembly in Arkansas	1917
Church of God	Herbert Armstrong	1933
Evangelical Church	Local Pastor	1950+
Calvary Chapel	Chuck Smith	1965

Introduction

This book is intended to be a short introduction to Catholic
Apologetics. Apologetics doesn't mean apologizing for being a
Catholic. Apologetics comes from the Latin word apologia
which means reasoned defense. Catholic Apologetics deals
with the reasonable defense of the Catholic Faith. This book
contains a series of chapters to help you learn about the Faith.
You can also use it to defend the Faith if someone asks, "Why
do Catholics do or believe _____?"

When Jesus ascended into Heaven, he didn't leave a book
behind for Christians to know about what He taught. Jesus left
11 men to carry on the Church that He founded. This Church
went out and spread the good news that Jesus died for our
sins, was resurrected and ascended into Heaven.
If you come to believe that Jesus is God you have been saved.
This is the beginning of the process of salvation which requires
Baptism and more to maintain your salvation. The Early
Christians were expected to lead holy lives and confess their
sins in Church to maintain their holiness. The first Christians
were Jews and already had organized ritual worship. The Early
Church evolved following the Jewish Synagogue model.

There is a group of writers known as the Early Church Fathers
that wrote about what the Early Christians were teaching and
doing before, they had a Bible. These writings give us great
insight into how the Early Church evolved out of Judaism in the
first century.

It wasn't until the end of the 300s that the Early Catholic
Church assembled what we now call the Bible. There are
hundreds of early Christian writings that give us insight into
how the Early Catholic Church interpreted the Bible before it
had a Bible.

The Catholic Gospel is summed up in Ephesians Chapter 2 verses 8-10. We are saved by God's Grace, through Faith in Jesus Christ unto the Good Works God has laid out for us.

This book utilizes the Jewish understanding of the Old Testament, the New Testament and the Early Church Fathers to explain the Catholic Faith.

This book is only a pail full of information from the vast beach of information about the Catholic Faith. Feel free to do your own exploring on the beach. There are many additional resources for further study at the end of this book.

1

Why You Should Be a Christian

First, we have to establish if there is a God. The God of Christianity is that which existed before time and space and therefore exists outside of time and space. God is the first cause, the one who started everything before time and space. Because God is outside of time and space He cannot be measured. We know God exists because everything we can sense exists and it all had to come from something. You could think of God as the source of the Big Bang. Some people try to get around the Big Bang theory of the origin of the universe by proposing there are an infinite number of previous or parallel universes that keep regenerating themselves. None of these previous or parallel universes can be measured, just like God cannot be measured. Others propose the beginning of the universe developed from subatomic ether or quantum field. Neither of these theories allow the development of something from nothing. They still require something to start with. You can choose to put your Faith in God or in universes proposed by science that cannot be measured by science. Choose wisely.

At some point in time God gave two human beings an infinite soul so that they would be made in the Image and Likeness of God. God gave them free will to choose to love Him back. When they decided to disobey God, He expelled them from the garden that He gave them to live in and made them work the ground for the rest of their existence. We inherit their fallen nature as "original sin" which is the lack of God's Grace that we are born in not actual sin. This fallen nature is the reason we sometimes choose to do the wrong thing. Our bad choices are source of evil and results in misery for others. God's plan is for us to love Him so we can be with Him in Heaven after our time here on earth. God's gift of love for us is constantly offered to us but we have to choose to accept to love God back. Dying isn't the worst thing that can happen to us. Dying without a loving relationship with God is the worst thing that could happen to a person.

Later, God revealed Himself to Noah when He told him to build an ark to save the animals and Noah's family. There is ample evidence to demonstrate a worldwide flood. Later, God Revealed Himself to Abraham when He told Abraham to leave the land of Ur and go to a place that God would show him. By Faith Abraham left Ur and God rewarded him by making his descendants as numerous as the stars in the sky through his son Isaac. Isaac had a son named Jacob whose name was changed to Israel after he wrestled with God (Gen ch32). Jacob/Israel had 12 sons who became the leaders of the 12 tribes of Israel who ended up in Egypt.

Later, God revealed Himself to Moses. When Moses asked, "Who shall I say sent me?" God answers "Tell them I Am sent you" because God is the one who simply exists outside of time and space. God guided Moses to lead the descendants of Abraham out of Egypt to the promised land now known as Israel. God gave Moses the Ten Commandments and the laws in the book of Leviticus to govern His chosen people.

At the right time God sent His son Jesus to restore our relationship with Him. The Roman Empire brought peace, reliable communication and travel to a large part of the known civilized world. Civilized people spoke Greek or Latin which made it easier to spread the Gospel.

3

Jesus' death and resurrection was the final sacrifice that allows us to restore our relationship with God.

The fact that Jesus died, and was resurrected   is recorded in the first century by the Roman historian Tacitus and Jewish historian Josephus who could never account for the empty tomb. Jesus' resurrection was witnessed by women, His Disciples and over 500 other witnesses. Jesus' resurrection is recorded within 5 to 10 years which is historically too short of a time for a myth to develop. Jesus' Apostles and many other early Christians died willingly rather than give up their Faith in Jesus Christ. Their unshakable Faith in Jesus caused many other people to become Christians. Christianity was illegal for over 250 years but continued to grow year after year.

When Jesus ascended into Heaven, He left a Church behind to carry on His teaching. That Church was headed by the Apostle Peter who ended his days in Rome. The Apostles taught and ordained Bishops who passed on the Faith when the Apostles moved on to another city or died. The Early Christians learned the Faith from the Tradition and Teaching of the Bishops who read the Greek translation of the Old Testament called the Septuagint and the Memoirs of the Apostles that eventually became the New Testament. The Catholic Church did not assemble the Bible as we have it today until the end of the 300s. Jesus left behind a Church not a book. This Church was known as the Catholic Church by 107AD when Ignatius of Antioch refers to it in his letter to the Smyrnaeans.

The best reason to become a Christian is for your own happiness. When we discover that things can't make us happy, we find that happiness comes from God who loved us enough to give us life. This allows us to first love ourselves, which then allows us to love others, which leads us to God who loved us first.

Why You Should Go to Church

God is the Creator of the Universe and us, so He is worthy of our Praise and Worship. Every civilization that recognizes a god offers that god praise and worship as a community.

The same God that created everything gave Moses the 10 Commandments, which required the Israelites to rest as a nation on the Sabbath which is Saturday and to keep it Holy. God sent His only Son Jesus to die and be resurrected for our salvation. From the beginning Christians started worshiping on the Lord's Day, the day of resurrection, which is Sunday. All Christians, who are part of the Body of Christ through Baptism (1 Cor ch12), are expected to offer Praise and Worship to God on Sunday as part of the Body of Christ, His Church.

Protestant worship services follow two general patterns. The Lutheran churches, the Anglican church and its off-shoots have a similar worship service to the Catholic Mass. Others use the worship pattern developed by John Calvin that starts with a hymn, then a Bible reading and a long sermon about the reading, followed by another hymn. These churches celebrate the Lord's Supper once a

5

month or maybe a few times per year. Other Protestant churches have a more varied worship service with a lot of music and praise songs.

The Catholic Mass evolved out of the Jewish worship already in existence at the time of Christ. This is why it is not specifically laid out in the Bible. The Bible is the collection of inspired writings that the Catholic Church later decided could be read at Mass. The Catholic Mass is divided into two parts; the Liturgy of the Word and the Liturgy of the Eucharist. During the Liturgy of the Word we receive four Bible readings and a homily on how to apply them in our lives. During the Liturgy of the Eucharist, the bread and wine are transformed into the Body and Blood of Jesus for our salvation. This is only available in the Catholic and Orthodox Churches but not in the various Protestant churches.

Catholics have the opportunity to Praise and Worship God on the Lord's Day and to receive the Eucharist. The Eucharist is the Body and Blood of Jesus in the form of bread and wine. John's Gospel (ch6) is where Jesus tells us we must eat His flesh and drink His blood. Jesus said at the Last Supper Passover meal that the bread was His Body and the wine was His Blood. Jesus' words are plain and simple in the Gospels of Matthew (ch26), Mark (ch14) and Luke (ch22) as well as Paul's letter to the Corinthians (chs 10 and 11). See the chapter in this book on the Eucharist for more information. The Eucharist is a great source of Grace if properly received and can help us grow in Holiness. During the Mass, our worship is combined with the Angels and Saints in Heaven as described in the book of Revelation by the Apostle John (ch4,5,19). The Catechism discusses our Sunday obligation to attend Mass in section 2180.

The Catholic Church is full of Christians growing in holiness. Some are further along than others. Going to Church doesn't make you Holy, but the Catholic Church provides a path to Holiness if you will follow it. Everything the Catholic Church teaches is logically for our own good if you research it.

In the Lord's Prayer we ask God to forgive our sins as we forgive others. If you are not willing to forgive your fellow members in the Body of Christ, then you cannot expect God to forgive you for your trespasses. Forgiveness for past hurts is the first step back into the Body of Christ, His Church.

The Eucharist will not benefit a person in a state of mortal sin, so if you haven't been to confession in a long time, take advantage of this sacrament before receiving the Eucharist. The Mass is a source of Grace to be a light of salvation for the whole world. Take advantage of it and be a good example of a Christian for others to follow.

The Evolution of Judaism into Catholic Christianity

There were many things that the early Christians adopted from first century Judaism. The first Christians were Jews that recognized Jesus as the Messiah. Gentiles weren't added until 5 or 10 years later. Evangelism was done through the Jewish Synagogue network. The first Christians adapted the Friday mini Passover and Sabbath worship into Mass on Sunday. They also adopted the Jewish offices in the Synagogue. The Ruler of the Synagogue became the Bishop and the Servant of the Synagogue became the Deacon. As the Christian communities grew and the Bishop couldn't perform the Mass at all of his Churches, the office of Priest was added to perform some of the sacraments that the Bishop performed. The early Christian communities adopted the care of the widows, sick and poor like the Synagogue communities.

You could be expelled from the Christian community for major sins just like you could be expelled from the Synagogue community. The early Christians used the Greek Septuagint translation for the Old Testament Scripture like the Diasporate Jews (Jews that lived in areas outside of Jerusalem) did. The Diasporate Jews were more accepting of Christianity than the Palestinian Jews because they were influenced by Greek philosophy. The early Christians kept the Moral Jewish Law as specified by Jesus (Matt ch16) but dismissed the Ceremonial Law (Acts ch15) that Jesus rejected. Circumcision evolved into Baptism for initiation into the community. The Jewish sect known as the Essenes had a sacred meal involving bread and wine and was a

8

community of celibate men which provided a model for communities of Monks later on.

There was no single group of Jews that became the early Christians, but many Jewish Priests and Pharisees became Christians. Jesus did criticize the Jewish leaders that rejected Him but He also praised those that recognized Him. The Jews celebrated a Passover like meal on Friday. During the Last Supper, Jesus evolved this Todah (Thanksgiving) meal into the Catholic Liturgy of the Eucharist. During the Synagogue worship service on Saturday, the Jews would begin with a Call to Prayer called the Shema, "Hear O Israel the Lord your God is One". This would be followed by prayers and petitions to God. Then there would be readings from the Torah. Followed by readings from the Prophets and histories. A sermon would follow encouraging imitation of what is taught by the readings. Then there would be Psalms of praise to God, followed by prayers asking for God's blessing. The Synagogue service would end with the Aaronic blessing: "May the Lord bless you and keep you; May His face shine upon you and be gracious to you; May the Lord lift up his countenance upon you and give you peace." This Jewish form of worship developed into the Catholic Liturgy of the Word.

The Early Christians combined the two worship services of the Jews to become our Mass on Sunday. Acts chapter 2 describes how the early Christians gathered on the first day of the week called the Lord's Day which is Sunday. Sunday worship is established in the Didache about 70AD.

9

Early Christian worship on Sunday is described by Justin Martyr in 155AD in his first Apology starting at chapter 65. In 215AD Hippolytus of Rome wrote down many of the early Church practices including what they did when they gathered for Mass on Sundays.

This is a brief description of the Jewish practices that evolved into Christian practices. Jews held a Passover like meal on Friday and worshiped on Saturday. Catholics continue to offer the combined Friday and Saturday Jewish traditions on Sunday. The Jews had an ordered way to worship and many Christian churches follow the ordered worship procedure of the early Christians. Today the Jews keep the Word of God in the Tabernacle. Catholics keep the Word made Flesh called the Eucharist in the Tabernacle. Jews stand during the reading of the Torah (first 5 books of Moses). Catholics stand during the Gospel readings. The Jews brought their boys into covenant with God after 8 days. Catholics bring our babies into covenant with God through Baptism. Synagogues had two offices: The Ruler of the Synagogue became the Bishop and the Servant of the Synagogue became the Deacon in the Early Church. Synagogue communities cared for their members and Christian communities continue to care for their members today. The Jews used incense to represent our prayers rising to God and Catholics continue to use incense for the same reason. The Jews confessed their sins to a Priest and then offered something in atonement their sins. Catholic Priests continue to hear confessions and repentant sinners do something for penance in atonement for their sins. The Jewish priests wore decorated robes when performing their duties on God's behalf. Catholic Clergy continue to wear decorated robes when celebrating the

Mass. The Jews that lived outside of Jerusalem prayed three times a day facing Jerusalem. The Didache required the Early Christians to pray the Lord's Prayer three times a day. The Jews fasted on Tuesday and Thursday. The Didache required the Early Christians to fast on Wednesday and Friday. We are still required to fast or offer something else in penance on Fridays. The Jews had the Sanhedrin to decide matters of law. The Catholic Church started holding Councils to determine matters of Church practice from the beginning. This is first recorded in the Book of Acts chapter 15 at the Council of Jerusalem where the Apostles discussed and decided how much of the Jewish Law was still binding on Christians.

From all of this we can see that Catholic Christianity is an evolution of first century Judaism. We are the Church that existed from the beginning and picked the books that would later become the Bible. Since the New Testament was still being written, the Early Christians didn't start a new religion from scratch, they modified their Jewish religion into the New Covenant Christianity.

It wasn't until the late 1800s that the anti-Semitic Adolf von Harnack first proposed that Christianity developed apart from Judaism.

The Church That Jesus Left Behind to Carry on His Mission

Many people assume that Jesus left us a book as an authority and not a teaching Church. The writings of the New Testament, that both Protestants and Catholics agree are Scripture, tell us that Jesus didn't leave us a book.

In Matthew chapter 16 we learn that Jesus said "You are Peter and, on this Rock, I will build my Church". He gives Peter the keys to the kingdom indicating his authority in the kingdom and that it would be handed on to successors like ministers that served the Jewish kings (Isiah ch22). This is a transfer of authority from the seat of Moses in the Old Covenant to the new seat of authority in the New Covenant, the Chair of Peter. Jesus gives Peter and the Apostles the power to bind and loose, showing that they had authority to make and discontinue laws and the fellowship of members of the Church. After His resurrection Jesus gives the Apostles the authority to forgive or retain sins (John ch20). In Matthew chapter 28, before ascending into Heaven, Jesus tells the Apostles that all the authority that God gave Him, he passes onto the Apostles. Jesus also told the Apostles to go out and teach the world everything that He taught and to Baptize them in the Father, Son and Holy Spirit. Jesus promises to be with them until the end of the age.

In John's Gospel chapter 17 Jesus prays that we would all be one as He and the Father are one. This tells us that Jesus wants there to be unity in the Church, not thousands of conflicting denominations. The end of John's Gospel chapters 20 and 21 tells us that everything is not written in what we now call the Bible because no book could hold it all. The Bible is the collection of books that the Catholic Church assembled and established that these are the inspired texts that can be read at Mass in 382Ad at the earliest. This tells us that Jesus left a Church not a book.

In the Book of Acts chapter 1, Peter and the rest of the Apostles meet to replace Judas as one of the 12 Apostles. The King James Bible tells us that they referred to Judas' office as a 'Bishopric'. The understanding from the beginning is that the Apostles hold an office that has successors.

In the Book of Acts chapter 2 Peter preaches to the Jews and 3,000 are added to the Church through Baptism. This shows that the Church that Jesus left behind to carry on His mission existed before the New Testament was written. Jesus left a Church not a book.

The Book of Acts chapter 9 uses the Greek phrase, "ekklesia kath holos," which means "the Church throughout all". From this we derive the name Catholic Church meaning the whole group of called out people that believe the same universal thing.

The Book of Acts chapter 15 tells us at the Council of Jerusalem, the Apostles, and those they had appointed called presbyters, held a Council. That Council made a decision that was binding on all Christians that went against what was then considered Scripture. The Old Testament required all the followers of God to be circumcised (Gen ch17). This shows that the Apostles knew that they had authority from Jesus that could bind

13

and loose the laws of the old covenant before there was a Bible. Their decree to the Church says, "It seems good to the Holy Spirit and to us .... "

This shows that the Church had binding authority and was protected by the Holy Spirit as Jesus promised. They sent the decree out with Paul, Barnabas and other appointed messengers, showing how the authority came from the Apostles not a private interpretation of the Bible by individuals.

When the Apostles went out and founded Churches, they would appoint successors that we now call Bishops by laying hands on them. In 1 Timothy chapter 3 Paul tells Timothy that the Church is the Pillar and Foundation of Truth not the Bible which was still being written. In chapter 4 Paul tells Timothy to be a good minister, to teach soundly and to not neglect the gift he was given through the laying on of his hands. Paul reminds him again in 2 Timothy 1:6 "Remember the gift you received with the laying on of my hands" referring to when he made Timothy a Bishop. Paul also warns Timothy to be careful about whom he lays hands on and be sure they know and follow the Faith before laying hands on them. This shows how the Faith was passed on through the teachers not just a book. In Ephesians chapter 4, Paul also lists the different positions in the Church like prophets, teachers, readers etc. In Titus chapter 1, Paul reminds Titus that he left him in Crete to teach the people rightly and to appoint presbyters in every town to properly hand on the Faith. Paul also tells Titus that the men he appoints should teach and appoint other men following what we now call Apostolic Succession. In 1 Corinthians chapter 10 and 11, Paul tells the Corinthians

14

of the Church practices and that we have no other practices and neither do the Churches of God. Unity in practice was expected among the Christians then and now.

These Bible passages speak of the Unity that God desires for His Church.
Romans 12:4-5 "For as in one body we have many members, and the members do not all have the same function, so we, though many, are one body in Christ, and individually members one of another"

1 Corinthians 1:10 "I appeal to you, brothers, by the name of our Lord Jesus Christ, that all of you agree, and that there
be no divisions among you, but that you be united in the same mind and the same judgment."

Acts 4:32 "Now the full number of those who believed were of one heart and soul, and no one said that any of the things that belonged to him was his own, but they had everything in common."

Hebrews 13:11 "Let brotherly love continue"

Ephesians 4:5-6 "One Lord, one faith, one baptism, one God and Father of all, who is above all and through all and in all.

All of these verses speak about the unity that God wants for His Church.

15

John 17:21 "That they may all be one. As you, Father, are in me and I am in you, may they also be in us, so that the world may believe that you have sent me.

The many conflicting teachings in the various Protestants do not demonstrate much unity. When to Baptize and what Baptism does is a fundamental basic doctrine concerning salvation on which there is no agreement.

In 90AD the Church in Corinth had a dispute, so they wrote a letter to the Bishop of Rome. Pope Clement, Bishop of Rome wrote back that the Apostles received their authority from Jesus and the Bishops received their authority from the Apostles. We call this handing down of authority Apostolic Succession. When the Corinthians had a dispute, they wrote to the Church in Rome and not Jerusalem, Antioch, another nearby major Church or the Apostle John, because they knew that Rome had the Authority.

In 107AD Ignatius Bishop of Antioch writes that the teachings of the Church are passed on through the Bishops not a book. Ignatius also tells us that wherever the Bishop is, there is the catholic Church. In his letter to the Church in Rome, Ignatius writes that he doesn't command them like Peter and Paul, but asks them not to try and rescue him when he gets there. This is early evidence that the Church in Rome had the teaching of Peter and Paul because this was the last place that they lived and taught.

In 150AD the early Church historian Hegesippus took a trip from Jerusalem to Rome by land. He writes that the teachings of the Church are passed on through the

Bishops. He writes that the Church teaches the same thing in Jerusalem, Corinth and Rome. This shows that from the beginning there was unity in the Church teaching and practice not the 'variety' that some propose.

In 180AD Irenaeus, Bishop of Lyon in Gaul (France), wrote a 5-volume book against Heresies. Irenaeus learned the Faith from Polycarp, Bishop of Smyrna, who learned the Faith from the Apostle John. Irenaeus writes that if two Churches have a doctrinal dispute, they need to see which Church can trace its history back to an Apostle. Or he writes, all you have to do is find out what the Church in Rome teaches, since all Churches have to be in agreement with that Church because Peter and Paul taught there.

All of this tells us that the Church that Jesus left behind was known as the Catholic Church and was headquartered in Rome by the end of the first century. Unity can only be maintained through authority. The Catholic Church has the Authority from Jesus and is protected from error, through the Holy Spirit, like Jesus said it would be (Matt chs 16 and 28).

The Catholic Church offers the authority of the Chair of Peter, the Church Councils and the Bible to guide us as we grow in our Faith in Jesus Christ.

17

Development of Christian Worship

Jewish Worship 30AD	Mass 155AD by Justin Martyr	Modern Catholic Mass
Synagogue Sabbath Worship	Lord's Day Sunday Worship	Saturday and Sunday Worship
Begin with Call to Prayer Hear O Israel the Lord your God is One	On the day we call the day of the sun, we all gather in the same place.	Greeting of the Assembly In the name of the Father, Son and Holy Spirit.
This is followed by some prayers and petitions asking God to bless His people		Penitential Act: I confess... and or, Lord have Mercy, Christ have Mercy. Glory to God in the Highest.
Then there would be readings from the 5 books of Moses called the Torah	The writings of prophets are read as long as time permits.	Old Testament reading, Psalms and New Testament reading.
Readings from the Prophets and historic writings of the scriptures	The memoirs of the Apostles are read as long as time permits.	Gospel reading where we stand out of reverence for the Word of God.
The presider would then offer a sermon encouraging imitation of the readings.	When the Reader has finished, the presider encourages them to imitate these things.	Homily explaining the readings and encouraging their imitation in our current life.
Then they would sing Psalms of praise to God.		Profession of Faith with the Apostle or Nicaean Creed
Followed by prayers asking for God's blessings.

The Worship service would end with the Aaronic blessing: | We all rise together and offer prayers for ourselves and others, so that we may be found faithful to the commandments, and to obtain eternal salvation. | Prayers of the Faithful where we pray to God for blessings for ourselves and others that we may live in communion with Him and obtain eternal life. |

May the Lord bless you and keep you; May His face shine upon you and be gracious to you; May the Lord lift up his countenance upon you and give you peace."	When the prayers are concluded we exchange the kiss.	This is the Sign of Peace now exchanged at the end of the Eucharistic Liturgy
Friday Sabbath Preparation is a Mini Passover in the Home that is a Todah or Thanksgiving Sacrifice.	Then someone brings bread and a cup of water and wine mixed together to him that presides over the brethren.	Presentation of Gifts when the Bread and Wine and money collected for the Church are brought forth to the Altar.
Cakes of unleavened bread and wine are used along with prayers to offer thanks to God in the home Synagogue with the eldest male acting as the presider.	The presider takes them and prays over them so that the food which is blessed by the prayer is trans-mutated into the flesh and blood of that Jesus who was made flesh.	The Priest or Bishop acts in the Person of Christ and recites the words of Jesus over the Bread and Wine and transforms them into the Body, Blood, Soul and Divinity of Jesus Christ
A Todah Sacrifice could be offered by someone whose life had been delivered from peril, disease, or the sword to show his gratitude to God.	When he has concluded the prayers and thanksgivings, all present give voice to an acclamation by saying "Amen"	The Eucharistic Prayer is concluded by the Faithful acclaiming the Great Amen. Who prepare to receive the Body and Blood of Christ.
The bread and meat, along with wine, would constitute the elements of the sacred Todah meal, which would be accompanied by prayers and songs of thanksgiving, such as Psalm 116	When the presider has given thanks and the people have responded, the Deacons give the "eucharisted" bread, wine and water. The Deacons also take the bread to those who are absent.	The Eucharistic Bread and Wine is then distributed to the Faithful present at the Mass. Some people are authorized to take the Eucharistic Bread to those that cannot attend.

The Short History of the Bible

The Bible is the collection of writings that the Catholic Church decided were inspired and could be read at Mass. It is a collection of books written by different authors in different writing styles, over thousands of years, for different audiences. The Bible contains historical events, but it is not written like a history book. It is not a manual on how to run a religion or build a church. Those things already existed before the Bible was assembled. The Teaching of the Twelve Apostles called the Didache is the earliest manual on how to run a Church. In modern times the Catholic Church is governed by Canon Law and the Catechism which are based on Scripture.

At the time of Jesus, the Sadducees, that taught and worshiped at the Temple in Jerusalem, considered only the 5 books of Moses to be the word of God. The Pharisees and Rabbis that taught and worshiped in the Synagogues, considered the 5 books of Moses, the writings of the Prophets, the Psalms, and some of the historical writings as Scripture. They grouped these writings in sets of 22 or 24 books. The Essene Jews had another set of writings that they used in their community. The Jews of this time did not have a standardized Old Testament.

Jews living outside of Jerusalem used a Greek Translation of the Old Testament called the Septuagint. This translation has the 46 books of the Catholic Old Testament in it, and a few others that did not make it into the Catholic Old Testament. The 7 books that are in the Catholic Old Testament but not the Protestant Old Testament are 1st and 2nd Maccabees, Wisdom, Baruch, Sirach, Tobit, and Judith.

The Early Christians considered the Greek Septuagint version of the Hebrew writings as Scripture. The New Testament quotes from the Greek Septuagint version of the Old Testament more than 80% of the time. All the books that made it into the New Testament were written in the first century. This is a basic history of the Bible.

Around 90AD a rabbinic school in Jamnia had a debate on which books were sacred and generally concluded that the Song of Songs and Ecclesiastes were inspired texts.

Rabbi Akiba Ben Joseph started standardizing the writings that the Jews would use in their Synagogues between 100 and 130AD. This collection is known as the Tanakh. He declared that the book of Sirach and all others written after that do not defile the hand which means they were not sacred texts that could not be touched after they were written. He established a canon of 22 or 24 books depending on how they were organized. The current Protestant Old Testament of 39 books is a reorganization of the 24 books. The Jews that rejected Jesus settled their Old Testament 100 years after Christianity had been started by Jesus and carried on by Peter and the Apostles.

The Hebrew Masoretic Text commonly used today was developed between 500 and 900AD. The Hebrew scholars took the consonant only Hebrew text and added vowels to make whole words as we have them in modern books.

The oldest list of the New Testament books is on incomplete scrap of parchment known as the Muratorian fragment from around 170AD. It lists the Gospels of Mathew, Mark, Luke, and John, Acts of the Apostles, 1st and 2nd Corinthians, Ephesians, Philippians, Colossians,

Galatians, 1st and 2nd Thessalonians, Romans, Philemon, Titus, 1st and 2nd Timothy, Jude, 1st and 2nd John, Wisdom of Solomon, Revelation of John, and Revelation of Peter as scripture. This list does not include 1 and 2 Peter, James, 3 John and Hebrews.

In 180AD Irenaeus writes that there are only 4 Gospels and their authors are Matthew, Mark, Luke and John.

In 200AD Origen considered the 4 Gospels, the Book of Acts, the 14 letters of Paul, 1 Peter, Jude, 1 John and the Book of Revelation as Scripture. Origen expressed reservations concerning James, 2 Peter, 2 and 3 John. Origen also considered Gospel of Peter, Gospel of the Hebrews, Acts of Paul, I Clement, Epistle of Barnabas, Didache, and Shepherd of Hermas as divinely inspired.

Around 315AD Eucebius of Caesarea wrote about the Canon of Scripture based on what he learned from Origen's library and the libraries in Alexandria and Jerusalem. He wrote that the universally recognized books are the Gospels of Matthew, Mark, Luke and John, Book of Acts, the 14 Epistles of Paul (including Hebrews), 1 Epistle by Peter, 1 Epistle by John and the Revelation (Apocalypse) of John. Eucebius writes that these writings are accepted by some Churches but not all Churches: 2 Epistle of Peter, 2 and 3 Epistles of John, James and Jude. He writes that the Church in Rome rejects the book of Hebrews and many Churches read the Shepherd of Hermas during the Divine Liturgy. Eucebius writes that these books are non-Apostolic writings but useful for teaching: Acts of Paul, Shepherd of Hermas, Apocalypse of Peter, Epistle of Barnabas, Didache-Teaching of the 12 Apostles, Gospel of the Hebrews, and the Apocalypse of John.

Eucebius writes that these writings are heretical: Gospel of Peter, Gospel of Thomas, Gospel of Mathias, Acts of Andrew, and Acts of John. This shows that the New Testament list we have today was not finalized at this time.

Around 325AD the Codex Vaticanus, the Codex Sinaicticus and the Codex Alexandria were assembled. They are likely from the 50 copies of Scripture in Greek commissioned by the Roman Emperor Constantine. Between these 3 ancient books we have the fully accepted 66 book Old Testament, the books of the Deuterocanon (aka the apocrypha) including 3 Esdras, Wisdom, Prologue to Ecclesiasticus, Ecclesiasticus, Esther (with additions), Judith, Tobit, Baruch, Epistle of Jeremiah, Daniel (with additions), and the 1, 2, 3, and 4 Maccabees. They contain the New Testament Four Gospels, Book of Acts, 1 and 2 Peter, 1,2 and 3 John, Jude, James, the Epistle to the Hebrews the 13 Pauline Epistles, and John's Book of Revelation.

In 360AD the Council of Laodicea listed a canon of scripture that had 26 of the 27 books of the New Testament leaving off John's Book of Revelation.

In 367AD Bishop Athanasius of Alexandria listed the 27 books of the New Testament in his Church Calendar letter sent to his Churches in his area.

In 382AD Pope Damasus at the Council of Rome listed the 27 books of the New Testament and 46 books of the Old Testament as the Canon of Scripture for use in Churches.

In 383AD Pope Damasus commissioned St. Jerome to make a Latin translation of the New and Old Testament Scriptures. Jerome used the Hebrew texts for his Old

Testament translation and Greek writings for the New Testament translation. The Hebrew texts didn't include the Old Testament books that were in the Greek Septuagint because the Jews had rejected them. Jerome made a Latin translation of these books after they were confirmed by the Councils of Hippo and Carthage.

In 386AD St. Augustine guided the Council of Hippo in North Africa which established the same list of 46 Old Testament books and 27 New Testament books.

In 397AD the Council of Carthage under St. Augustine came up with the same list and sent it to Rome for approval after another council in 419AD.

In 405AD Pope Innocent I listed the 27 books of the New Testament and 46 books of Old Testament in his Church Calendar letter to the Bishop of Lyon in France.

In 434AD Vincent of Lerins wrote, "Since the canon of Scripture is complete, and sufficient for everything, what need is there to join with it the authority of the Church's interpretation? Because all do not accept it in one and the same sense. One understands its words in one way, another in another way producing various interpretations. Therefore, the right understanding should be in accordance with the standard of Ecclesiastical (Church) interpretation."

In 787AD the Second Council of Nicaea accepted the decrees of previous smaller Councils. This included the Canon of Scripture determined in 397 by the Council of Carthage.

In 1441 the Council of Florence approved the list of 46 Old Testament books and 27 New Testament books accepted by the Councils of Rome, Hippo and Carthage.

In 1550 the list of 46 Old Testament books and 27 New Testament books were made official at the Council of Trent.

This is why there is a difference today between the Catholic and Protestant Bibles. It wasn't until the end of the 300s that list of Old and New Testament Scriptures were established.

The Didache, the Shepherd of Hermas, 1st Clement to the Corinthians, and the Epistle of Barnabas were read in many early Churches. The Book of Revelation, 2 Peter, 2 and 3 John, Jude, James and the Book of Hebrews were considered questionable by many theologians and Churches.

The Catholic Church that teaches that baptism forgives sins, that Jesus is present in the Eucharist, and that the Bishop of Rome is the head of the Church, is the Church that decided which books were the divinely inspired Word of God. The Early Church Synods of Rome, Hippo and Carthage are the first Church councils that established the list of divinely inspired books. This list was confirmed at the Ecumenical Councils of 2nd Nicaea and Florence.

The Catholic Church hand copied the Bible for over 1100 years before moveable type was developed by Gutenberg. For the first 1500 years of Christianity the Bible was interpreted based on the Tradition handed on by the Apostles. This Tradition can be understood through the writings of the Early Church Fathers who had an overall majority understanding of the writings of the Old and New Testaments.

The Bible contains divinely inspired writings. But they need to be interpreted. The thousands of different Protestant churches have different interpretations of these divinely inspired writings. The Catholic Church has the oldest and original understanding of these writings. The Pope is the successor of the royal minister that Jesus left behind to feed His sheep and tend His flock (John ch21). This same Jesus promised to be with His Church to the end of time (Matt28:20). Jesus didn't leave us a book as an authority; He left us a Church to teach us what He taught the Apostles. Catholics put their trust in the Church that Jesus founded not a man's interpretation of the Bible that the Catholic Church assembled.

No Protestant church has a record of how they decided which books make up the New Testament; even Martin Luther said "What would we know of the Scriptures if it wasn't for the papists (Catholic Church)".

The Bible Alone is not in the Bible

Catholic Christians and Protestant Christians both agree that the Bible contains Sufficient information for our Salvation. Protestants often string verses together to support their doctrine. The Catholic Church uses the Whole Bible that the Catholic Church assembled. The Catholic Church interprets the Bible based on the interpretation and practices handed down by the Apostles, not some man's interpretation made up 1500 or more years later. Catholics use the Bible to defend the Faith because it is the Highest Authority that Protestants will accept. When Paul refers to Scriptures in the New Testament, he is referring to the Old Testament not the Whole Bible because it was not yet written and assembled.

In 2 Tim 3:16-17 Paul tells Timothy, "All scripture is inspired by God and is useful for teaching, for reproof, for correction, and for training in righteousness, so that everyone who belongs to God may be proficient, equipped for every good work." This is the first verse Protestants use to "prove" Sola Scriptura also known as the Bible Alone. These verses need to be read in context with the previous two verses of 3:14-15 "But as for you, continue in what you have learned and firmly believed, knowing from whom you learned it, and how from childhood you have known the sacred writings that are able to instruct you for salvation through faith in Christ Jesus. All scripture is inspired by God and is useful for teaching, for reproof, for correction, and for training in righteousness, so that everyone who belongs to God may be proficient, equipped for every good work." The Scriptures of Timothy's youth was the Old Testament. Likely it would have been the Greek Septuagint version of the Old Testament because Timothy lived outside of Jerusalem, had a Greek father and had a Jewish mother (Acts ch16). The Greek Septuagint Old Testament contains the books that the Protestants removed from their Old Testament. Paul tells us in 2 Thessalians chapter 2 to hold fast to the Traditions you have been taught by word of mouth or letter. Here Paul is telling us that not all the teachings are written.

The Bereans from Acts chapter 17, who searched the Scriptures daily to confirm Paul's teaching, also would have been using the Septuagint version of the Old Testament since they lived in a Greek city as well. In 1

27

Corinthians chapter 4 Paul warns the Corinthians not to go beyond what is written. Here Paul is not writing about going beyond what is written in the Scriptures. He is writing about those whose names are written in the Book of Life and how they are in there by the gift of God's Grace, so do not be proud of being in the Book of Life because you can be removed from the it as well (Rev 3:5). None of these verses in the Bible say we should go by the Bible alone.

The Apostle John writes in his Gospel at the end of chapter 20 "Now Jesus did many other signs in the presence of His disciples that are not written in this book. But these are written that you may come to believe that Jesus is the Messiah, the Son of God, and that through this belief you may have life in his name." At the end of Chapter 21, John writes "It is this disciple (John) who testifies to these things and has written them and we know that his testimony is true. There are also many other things that Jesus did, but if these were to be described individually, I do not think the whole world would contain the books that would be written." These verses tell us that everything that Jesus did and said are NOT written in the Bible. The teachings that are not written in the Bible were passed on through the Oral Apostolic Tradition. The Bible is the written part of the whole Apostolic Tradition.

In 434AD Vincent of Lerins wrote in his book The Catholic Faith Against All Heresies 2:5 "But here someone perhaps will ask, "Since the canon of Scripture is complete, and sufficient of itself for everything, and more than sufficient, what need is there to join with it the authority of the Church's interpretation? Because all do not accept it in one and the same sense, but one understands its words in one way, another in another; so that it seems to be capable of as many interpretations as there are interpreters. Therefore, the rule for the right understanding of the prophets and apostles should be framed in accordance with the standard of Ecclesiastical and Catholic interpretation."

The Catholic Church uses the Sacred Tradition that the Apostles handed down before there was a New Testament and the Catholic Church established the list of books that would make up the Sacred Scriptures. When there were disputes on interpretations of Scripture, Church Councils were held that gave binding decrees just like the first Church Council in Jerusalem (Acts ch15) that did not go by Scripture alone. The Pope gives approval to the Council decisions and also offers Papal encyclicals to guide the Church. These are the magisterial commentaries that were given over a thousand years before the start of any Protestant church.

A major question is how we know what the Sacred Tradition is? The Church Fathers, the Bishop of Rome, and other Bishops wrote about the Christian Faith from the beginning. If you start with what the Catholic Church teaches today, many doctrines can be traced all the way back to the beginning through the Bishops and Church Fathers. There are many viewpoints given by Church Fathers and Bishops that don't agree with the many doctrines of the Catholic Church. This can be reconciled by the fact the Jesus promised to be with His Church until the End of the Age (Matt ch28). Church Councils, like the first one in Jerusalem (Acts ch15), give Holy Spirit guided decrees on disputed doctrines making them binding on all of the faithful.

There will always be dissenters, but Jesus' Church will exist in every age. The Real Presence of Jesus in the

Eucharist and Baptismal Regeneration as entry into the Church are two great examples.

These 2 concepts can be connected to the Church Fathers and Bishops in every age. The Catholic Church interprets the Bible based on its 2000 years of study and practices of the early Christians and Theologians.

Most Protestants do not believe in the Real Presence of Jesus in the Eucharist. Some Protestants teach Baptismal Regeneration and others teach it is just a visible sign of a personal commitment to Jesus. This shows that Sola Scriptura doesn't maintain the unity of the Church that Jesus desired and promised would exist in every age. Which Protestant church correctly interprets the Bible on these two concepts, the Lutheran church or the Baptist church? It is plain to see that the Bible Alone is not sufficient for its interpretation. The LARGE variety of Protestant churches demonstrate that the Bible cannot interpret itself. Each one is based on their founder's interpretation of the Bible. Protestants usually follow the church that agrees with their own "holy spirit" guided understanding of the Bible. The various Protestant faith traditions have varied views on the interpretation of Scripture which conflict with each other. This shows that Sola Scriptura is not capable of providing the Unity that Jesus prayed for and they have not existed in every age (John ch17). Protestant churches do not agree on what Baptism does or when to do it. There are many other core concepts that Protestants don't agree on because their interpretations are based on claimed "holy spirit" guided decisions of individuals.

The Trinity is one, the Church is one. Jesus only left behind one Church with Peter as its head. That Church is still here today in the Catholic Church.

Baptism: The Universal Sacrament

Baptism is the one thing that unites all Christians, but there are a wide variety of views on Baptism. Some Christian Churches teach that Baptism forgives sins, makes you a member of the Body of Christ, His Church (1 Cor ch12, Matt ch28, John ch1, Acts ch2&22 and 1 Peter ch3) and is a source of Grace through the Holy Spirit. Other churches teach that baptism is just an outward sign of your inward change of heart and that you have decided to be a Christian. Some Churches teach that you should baptize your babies and others teach that you have to believe before you can be baptized, so a baby has to wait until they are old enough to choose for themselves. Some churches teach that baptism has to be done with full immersion, commonly called dunking. Other Churches teach that baptism can be done by immersion or pouring water on the head. Some Churches teach that baptism is only done in the name of the Father, Son and Holy Spirit. Other churches teach baptism is done in the name of Jesus only or the Creator, the Redeemer and the Sanctifier.

This is what the Bible teaches about Baptism. The Jews had ceremonial washing rituals to purify themselves before performing certain acts on the behalf of God, so Baptism was not a new idea for them. In Ezekiel chapter 36, when the Jews were returning to Jerusalem, Ezekiel sprinkles them clean with water so that they will be worthy of living in God's Holy city again. He also tells them that he will put a new heart in them, just as our modern Baptism is an appeal for a clean heart (1 Peter ch3).

Jesus Baptism is described in Matthew chapter 3, Mark Chapter 1 and Luke chapter 3 and John chapter 1. In these Gospels the Holy Spirit descends on Jesus in the form of a dove and a voice from Heaven announces "This is my Beloved Son". Jesus baptism in John chapter 1 gives us an example of what Jesus was talking about in John chapter 3 where Jesus tells Nicodemus "You must be born of water and the spirit". After this, Jesus and His disciples went out Baptizing. This clearly links being "Born Again" to water Baptism. In Titus 3:5 Paul tells us that we are saved by the washing of regeneration, again linking Baptism to being born again.

At Pentecost, just 50 days after the resurrection of Jesus, in Acts chapter 2 verse 38 Peter tells the Jews, "Repent and be baptized, every one of you, in the name of Jesus Christ for the forgiveness of your sins. And you will receive the gift of the Holy Spirit." Some Protestant faith traditions use this verse to justify Baptizing in the name of Jesus only. Since Jesus specified in Matthew chapter 28 to Baptize in the name of the Father, Son and Holy Spirit the Trinity is the correct formula. Peter refers to this Baptismal formula as the Baptism of Jesus. Verse 39 that follows says, "this gift is for you and your children". This is one of the reasons the early Christians baptized their infants. Verse 41 tells us that 3,000 were added that day to the Church, the Body of Christ through Baptism. This shows that from the beginning, entrance into the Church is through Baptism, not asking Jesus to be your Personal Lord and Savior. In Acts chapter 22 Ananias says to Paul, "Why do you wait, arise and be Baptized and wash away your sins." This shows that Baptism really does forgive previous sin.

In 1st Peter chapter 3, we read "Just as Noah and his family were saved through water, Baptism now saves you. Not the removal of dirt but an appeal for a clean heart." This shows that we are saved when we are

Baptized, it is not just an outward symbol of an inward change of heart. It also shows that Baptism is not for removing dirt on the outside, so it does not have to be done through immersion. The water is a symbol of the inward cleansing of our heart. Titus chapter 3 also tells us that we are made clean through Baptism.

In early Christian times, some people would put off their Baptism until they were near death so they could enter into Heaven without sin. The Church has always encouraged people to be Baptized early and live a holy life afterward.

There are many instances of preaching to adults in the New Testament, telling them to repent or believe or have faith before baptism to be saved. This makes sense for the adults who were being preached to. Children who receive baptism have no personal sin to repent of, but they do inherit the sin tendency of human beings from Adam and Eve who sinned in the Garden of Eden (1 Cor ch15). Baptism is an initial source of Grace to help us live a holy life.

In Acts chapter 10 Peter Baptizes Cornelius and his household. In Acts chapter 16 Paul Baptizes Lydia and her household. Both of these households would likely contain children because the Jews often lived in 3 or 4 generation households. In Colossians 2:11–12 Paul links circumcision as the seal of the Old Testament with Baptism as the seal of the New Testament. Jewish male babies did not have to accept the faith of their fathers to enter into covenant with God at 8 days old. They were brought into the covenant based on the faith of their parents. It was natural for the Jews to bring their babies into the Faith of the family. Baptism had an advantage over Jewish circumcision because it allowed both girls and boys to enter into a covenant relationship with God.

The Catholic Church recognizes three forms of Baptism. The ordinary form of Baptism is with water flowing over the head and in the name of the Father, Son, and Holy Spirit through immersion or pouring. The second form is Baptism by desire. If a person comes to Faith in Jesus and wishes to follow Him, but dies before water Baptism can be done, then that person has received the Baptism of desire. The thief on the cross in Luke chapter 23 is an example of the Baptism of desire. The third form is Baptism by blood. This is Baptism by martyrdom. If a person comes to Faith in Jesus and is killed for being a Christian before water Baptism, that person has received Baptism by blood. All people who come to Faith in Jesus, but are killed for being a believer before they have been water Baptized, are guaranteed to go to Heaven as a martyr for the Faith.

Baptism permanently marks you as a Christian and gives you an initial Grace to grow in holiness. It is up to the parents, God parents and the individual to continue to grow in holiness. The Faith and Salvation of a Christian is a developing process not a onetime event.

Around 70AD the earliest manual for Christianity, called the Didache, was written. The Didache specifies that Baptism is to be done in the name of the Father, the Son and the Holy Spirit. It allows for Baptism in living (flowing) water, standing (warm or cold) water, or by pouring water on the head. The Didache does not require a person to be immersed in water.
In 155AD Justin Martyr writes that we are regenerated (born again) through baptism.

In 180AD Irenaeus, who learned the Faith from Polycarp who learned the Faith from the Apostle John, wrote that we Baptize infants and that we are born again through Baptism.
In 210AD Origen of Alexandria wrote that the baptism of infants is a tradition handed down to us by the Apostles.
In 215AD Hippolytus of Rome wrote about baptizing infants and being born again through Baptism as a standard practice of the Church.
In 251AD at the Synod of Carthage they discussed baptizing infants and decided there was no need to wait until the 8th day. It was the heretical groups that wrote against infant baptism as the early Church was developing.

In the 1500s Luther and Calvin taught that we should baptize babies and that Baptism was a source of Grace. It wasn't until the 1600s that some Anabaptists started the new tradition of accepting the faith before Baptism and that it was just a symbol of a believer's decision

The Catechism of the Catholic Church teaches about Baptism in paragraphs 1213 to 1284. Briefly it explains that Baptism forgives all previous sin and incorporates a person into the Body of Christ, His Church. The Catholic Church also teaches that we are born again through Baptism where we die to sin and put on the holiness of Christ. The Church teaches that we are forever sealed by a spiritual mark showing that we belong to Christ. Baptism is done only once in a lifetime and allows us to share in the priesthood of Christ.

Baptism can be done by anyone with intent to perform the Sacrament in an emergency. The person baptizing is required to use the Baptismal formula of Father, Son and Holy Spirit while dunking or pouring water 3 times.

The Eucharist: Real Presence or "Real Symbol"

Catholics and Protestants have different views on the
Eucharist or the Lord's Supper as it is known in many
Protestant faith traditions. Protestants and some
Catholics have a hard time with Jesus' command that we
must eat His flesh and drink His blood.

To understand the Eucharist, we first have to know the
Jewish background behind it. In Genesis chapter 14, after
Abraham won a battle against 5 Kings in the land of
Canaan, he offered 10% of the spoils of battle to the
Priest/King of Salem named Melchizadek who offered
him bread and wine with his blessing. This is the first
time a blessing was given after a thanksgiving offering. In
Hebrew the word for thanksgiving is Todah. In Greek the
word for thanksgiving is Eucharistia. This is where the
English word Eucharist comes from.

Exodus chapter 12 tells how the Israelites celebrated the
first Passover before they left Egypt by killing a male un-
blemished lamb, and applying its blood to their door
frame. The Israelites then had to roast the lamb and eat
the lamb along with unleavened bread, bitter herbs and
wine. They did this while the angel of death passed over
their homes and didn't kill their first-born sons. If they
didn't eat the lamb, then the firstborn son would die.
After leaving Egypt the Israelites received the miraculous
bread from Heaven called Manna in the morning and
quail for flesh in the evening (Exodus ch16). The Manna
was their miraculous Daily Bread. The Israelites kept
some of the Manna in the Ark of the Covenant with the 10
Commandments and Aaron's staff.

Later the Israelites built the portable Temple, specified
by God to Moses in the book of Exodus chapter 26. This

Temple had a special Altar for the Bread of the Presence and a pitcher of wine in the Holy Place. This bread was called the bread of Angels or Face of God in Hebrew. This Altar was also present in the Temple built by Solomon and rebuilt by Herod. On the Day of Atonement (Yom Kippur), the Priests would take the Bread of the Presence out and show it to the faithful Jews while the Priests proclaimed 'Behold God's Love for You". It was not a great leap for the Jews to believe that God could be present in the bread.

In John's Gospel chapter 6, Jesus gives His Bread of Life speech. Jesus says, "I am the Bread of Life and the Bread that I will give is my Flesh." Later Jesus says, "You have to eat My flesh and drink My blood to have Eternal Life." All the Jews and the Disciples were scandalized by this saying. Everybody took Jesus seriously and left except for the 12 Disciples who also didn't understand. Judas decided at this time to betray Jesus because he didn't believe. It wasn't until the Last Supper that the Disciples understood how they were to eat His flesh and drink His blood. This is covered in Matthew Chapter 26, Mark Chapter 14, Luke Chapter 22 and by Paul in 1 Corinthians chapter 11. In every chapter Jesus says THIS IS My body about the bread, and THIS IS My blood about the cup of wine. The words are plain and easy to understand here.

In Luke chapter 24, we learn that after the crucifixion, 2 disciples on the road to Emmaus came to know Jesus when He blessed and shared the bread this is referred to as the "breaking of the Bread" which was the Eucharist. When Luke writes the Book of Acts, he refers many times to the "Breaking of the Bread" as a short cut referring to this Eucharistic meal.

In 1st Corinthians chapter 5 Paul writes "Christ our Passover Lamb has been sacrificed so let us keep the feast." This connects the first Passover lamb that had to be eaten to be saved, to Jesus the new Passover Lamb that we have to eat to be saved. In Revelation chapter 5 and onward, Jesus is also identified as the Lamb.

In 1st Corinthians chapter 10 Paul writes "The cup of blessing that we bless, is it not a participation in the blood of Christ? The bread that we break, is it not a participation in the body of Christ? Because the loaf of bread is one, we, though many, are one body, for we all partake of the one loaf. This shows the unity of the first Christians in the celebration of the Eucharist.

In 1st Corinthians chapter 11 Paul gives his account of the Last Supper where Jesus says the bread is His Body and the wine is His Blood. This is the earliest account of this event in Scripture. Jesus' words about His Body and Blood are again plain and easy to understand. Paul warns that if you are in a sinful state or don't recognize it as the Body and Blood of Jesus you compound your sin and that is why many are sick and dying. Paul also says "We have no other practices and neither do the Churches of God."

In the book of Hebrews, we learn about the once for all sacrifice of Jesus. The Catholic Church re-presents the sacrifice that Jesus started in the upper room on Holy Thursday and finished on the cross on Good Friday at Mass every day during the Eucharistic Prayer. It is the same sacrifice that Jesus performed but re-presented like the Jews re-presented the original Passover. The Eucharist is the Perfect Sacrifice that Christians have been celebrating from the beginning during the Breaking of the Bread.

The Didache from, 70AD, is the earliest rule of Faith for Christians. The Didache says the Eucharist is only for the Baptized believer because we don't give that which is Holy to the dogs (unbaptized non-believers).

In 107AD Ignatius of Antioch writes the Eucharist is the medicine of immortality because Jesus said if you eat My flesh and drink My blood you will have eternal life. Ignatius also says to have nothing to do with the heretics that don't believe the Eucharist is the flesh and blood of our Lord.

In 150AD Justin the Martyr writes the bread and wine are prayed over and are transformed into the flesh and blood of our Savior Jesus Christ and the Deacons take it to those who cannot attend. This shows Jesus is substantially present in the bread and wine because it can be transported. Jesus is not just present symbolically or spiritually only during the Mass. His presence exists as long as it still looks like bread and wine.

In 180AD Irenaeus explains the Eucharist has 2 realities earthly and Heavenly.

Around 400AD St. Augustine wrote, "The Bread which you see on the altar, having been sanctified by the word of God, is the Body of Christ. The chalice, or rather, what is in that chalice, having been sanctified by the word of God, is the Blood of Christ."

The Catechism of the Catholic Church discusses the Eucharist in parts 1322 through 1419 because it is so central to our Faith. All of the Christian Churches that trace their founding to an Apostle believe in the presence of Jesus in the Eucharist. This is the original Christian understanding available only in the Catholic and Orthodox Churches.

It wasn't until the 1500s that Martin Luther taught that Jesus was present under and around the bread and wine. John Calvin taught that Jesus was present spiritually during the Lords Supper only.

It was Ulrich Zwingli that first proposed that the presence of Jesus was "only symbolic" because he misunderstood the Greek understanding of 'symbol'. For the Greeks a "symbol" was a physical representation of a spiritual reality. Zwingli living 1500 years later misunderstood this by thinking that a "symbol" was just a reminder of an earlier reality.

Salvation as a Process

Catholic Christians and Protestant Christians both agree that Jesus death on the cross and resurrection provided enough Grace for us to be saved. The difference is in how that Grace is applied to us. Protestants teach that through Faith or Believing they receive imputed righteousness and <u>appear</u> Holy to God. The Catholic Church teaches that by Grace, through Faith and Baptism we receive intrinsic (actual) righteousness and are <u>made</u> Holy before God so that we can do the Works He has planned for us (Eph 2:8-10)

Protestants teach that works play no part in your salvation but can be a demonstration that a person is saved. Martin Luther misunderstood what kind of "works" Paul is talking about in Romans chapter 3 and

Galatians chapter 2. In both cases Paul is speaking to the Jews that are insisting that the new Gentile converts have to adopt the Jewish "works of the law" to be saved. In Acts chapter 15, at the Council of Jerusalem, the Apostles gave a binding decree that Gentiles do not have to be circumcised; they only need to abstain from food sacrificed to idols. This was a binding decree on all Christians but the Jewish Christians didn't always follow this. In the early 400sAD Augustine confirmed that Paul was referring to the Jewish ceremonial and food "works of the law" in his writings on Romans and Galatians.

In the early 1500s Martin Luther developed his new salvation theology because he couldn't accept that his sins were forgiven through the sacrament of reconciliation. He found verses in the Bible that taught salvation by Faith apart from "works of the law". The "law" referred to in these verses is the Jewish ceremonial law and kosher laws. Martin taught that saved people are "covered" by Jesus righteousness like snow over a dung hill. Luther taught that God sees Jesus' righteousness while we are still sinners. In Luther's book Bondage to the Will he taught that when we are born, either God or the devil will take over our lives and all we can do is submit to their will. Therefore, if God is controlling your life the only way you can lose your salvation is to deny God.

A generation later, John Calvin further developed Luther's new salvation theology. Calvin taught that since God is all powerful and knowing, He decides which people He creates are going to Heaven and which people are going to Hell from the beginning of time. This means that God creates some people just to send them to Hell. However, the Bible teaches that God wants all men to be saved (2 Peter ch3 and 1 Tim ch2). John taught that IF you are one of God's Elect then no matter what you do God will save you in the end. Calvin taught that all our punishment for sin was put on Jesus, so our sins are covered by Jesus' shed blood. This new theology makes God an unjust judge by punishing Jesus for our sins.

Both of these new theologies teach that you can't lose your salvation through sin if you are in the group of "saved people". This leads to the misunderstanding that Salvation is a "one time" event.

It was difficult to really know which people were in the "saved" group so in the early 1800s some more conservative Protestants developed a new way to determine if you were in the group of the "Elect". People who had an "emotional conversion experience" and accepted Jesus as their personal Lord and Savior must be one of the Elect and were guaranteed to go to Heaven no matter what sins they later committed.

This new theology was promoted in the 1900s by groups like the Azusa Street Revival and the Billy Graham Crusades that appealed to people to have a conversion experience and give their lives to Christ. These people are now known as the Born-Again Christians that teach Once you are Saved you are Always Saved. However, giving your life to Christ is a start but not the end of the salvation process.

Adam and Eve were born with God's Grace and free will to choose to love God. When they chose to disobey God, they were expelled from the garden. We are all descendants of Adam and Eve and are now born without God's Grace. We inherit their fallen nature and are therefore prone to sin. This is referred to as "original sin" but is something missing not something inherited. The

Hebrews became God's chosen people through Abraham. The Hebrews through Abraham's son Isaac, and grandson Jacob/Israel, eventually ended up in Egypt. Moses led the Israelites out of Egypt and were given the Law of God, first through the 10 Commandments and then through the Laws of the book of Leviticus. If the Israelites sinned, they had to offer something back to God to be reconciled back to God. At the right time, God sent Jesus to bring the Jews back to Him, but some Jews have hardened hearts and refuse to recognize Jesus as their Messiah. Jesus sacrifice, started at the Last Supper and finished on the cross, is the final sacrifice that provides sufficient Grace to save all people, Jew or Gentile (Heb ch10, 1 Tim ch2)

After his encounter with Jesus, Paul writes about how we are saved by God's Grace through Faith in Jesus Christ, unto the Works He has set out for us to do as written in Ephesians 2:8-10. We are not saved by following the Levitical Code of the Jews.

The Early Christians were incorporated into the Body of Christ through Baptism (Matt ch28, John ch3, Acts ch2&9, 1Peter ch3 and 1Cor ch12). They still had to follow the 10 Commandments and do the works of mercy specified by Jesus in Matthew chapters 6,11 and 25.

They also had to avoid the sins listed in 1 Corinthians chapter 6 and Galatians chapter 5. If they sinned, they would have to confess their sins and do the specified penance to restore their relationship with Jesus and His Church (John ch20 James ch5). The Early Christians understood that you grow in Holiness through the Grace made available through the Sacraments.

Like the thief on the cross, salvation can occur at a specific point in time when you are drawn by God's Grace to Faith in Jesus and be completed if you die at that point in time. This is the initial righteousness Paul talks about in Romans chapter 4, but not the perfected sanctification he talks about in Romans chapter 2. If the person lives beyond the time of initial salvation, there is more to be done. This is because a personal relationship with Jesus develops over time. Jesus in Luke chapter 19, James in chapter 2 and Paul in Romans chapter 4 and Galatians chapter 3, use Father Abraham as the example of Faith. His story in Genesis takes from chapter 12 to chapter 24. Abraham is required to do many things and after each one is counted as righteous. This shows that salvation is a process as you continue to live in Faith with God.

After initial salvation we need to be Baptized to enter into the Covenant with God (Acts ch2). Children can enter into that same Covenant if they have parents and God parents that promise to bring that child up in the Faith. Through Baptism, we are incorporated into the Body of Christ (1 Cor ch12), made Holy by washing away all previous sin (Acts ch2 and 22), and are given an initial source of Grace to overcome the tendency to sin inherited from Adam and Eve. This state of Holiness is maintained through the Sacrament of Reconciliation (Confession) where future mortal sins are forgiven and reconciled though penance. Venial sins are forgiven through contrition, prayer, Bible study, Holy Water (that is why we bless ourselves when we enter the Church), and receiving the Eucharist. As we grow in understanding, we receive more Sacraments like the Eucharist and the Sacrament of Confirmation where Catholics choose to follow the Faith and are strengthened through the Holy Spirit so we can continue to live Holy lives and maintain our Salvation. All the penance due to sin that was not completed before death is completed in purgatory before entering Heaven because nothing unclean can enter there (Rev ch21 and Heb ch12).

Free Will allows us to walk away from the Body of Christ at any time and lose our Salvation up until death. We can also turn back to God at any time and be saved up until death. This is demonstrated in the story of the prodigal son from Luke chapter 15. The prodigal son takes his inheritance (salvation) and goes off to a far land and lives a sinful life spending his inheritance (losing his salvation). When he repents and returns to his father, his father welcomes him back with a party (restoring his salvation). The prodigal son offers to work as a servant for his father for his penance.

The Catholic Church teaches that Works are part of the salvation process which when done while in a state of Grace, are for the Glory of God. We can merit more Grace for works done while members of the Body of Christ because we are following God's plan for us and we will not lose our reward (Matt ch10). The Works that we must do are in Matthew chapters 6, 11, and 25; Mark chapter 16; Luke chapters 6 and 15; and John chapters 14 and 17. Jesus says we will be judged by our Works at the Final Judgment (Matt ch25) and those without works will be turned away because He never knew them (Matt ch7).

Faith is a process and our Salvation is an ongoing state that is maintained as long as we keep ourselves in a State of Grace and therefore a part of the Body of Christ. Our goal should be to continually conform our lives to the life of Christ and grow in holiness.

Salvation by Faith or Believing Alone?

Believing is the beginning of salvation, but not the end.
There are many verses in the Bible that say we are saved
by Believing or Faith. They are parts of preaching given
by the Apostles to bring people to Christ. There are also
many verses that teach what we must do after our initial
salvation. The Catholic Church uses the Whole Bible, not
just the verses that support the theology developed by
Martin Luther or John Calvin in the 1500s.

Ephesians 2:8-10 is a condensed version of the Catholic
understanding of Salvation, through Grace, Faith and
Works. James chapter 2 tells us that Believing and Faith
are not enough to save a person. Works are required as
well.

Romans chapter 2 tells us that it is <u>not</u> the hearers of the
law that will be saved but the <u>doers</u> of the law that will be
saved. The early Christians were required to do more
than just believe. The Didache, which is the teaching of
the 12 Apostles from 70AD, required Christians to live
morally and do the works of mercy that Jesus said they
had to do.

 The Catholic Church does teach that Belief and Faith are
necessary. In fact, if you come to believe in Jesus and get
killed right away, the Catholic Church teaches that you
are saved. The Catholic Church teaches that believing is a
process of growing in Faith to continue our salvation.
Father Abraham is the example of Faith used by Jesus
(John ch8), James (ch2), and Paul (Rom ch4). Abraham's
story takes place in Genesis chapters 12 through 24
which shows Salvation is a process, not a one-time event.
Abraham had to leave the land of Ur, circumcise himself
and all the men in his tribe, offer his son as a sacrifice and

give 10% of the spoils of battle to the Priest/King Melchizedek. After each event in the story of Abraham, God declared him righteous. This shows that Faith begins at one point and matures over time.

In the Catholic Church we start with coming to a belief that Jesus died for our sins and was resurrected. After learning about the Faith or receiving a promise from our parents to raise us in the Faith, we can then be baptized. After learning more about the Faith, we are allowed to receive the Eucharist, which is the real presence of Jesus under the appearance of Bread and Wine. After coming to a mature understanding of the Faith, we receive the Sacrament of Confirmation where we are sealed by the Holy Spirit and choose to follow in the Faith tradition that we have been raised in. We are inspired to believe through God's Grace when come Faith in Jesus Christ which equips us to do the Works that God has set out for us to do (Eph 2:8-10).

Some people think that if you do more good than bad God will let you into Heaven. If a person learns the whole truth of the Bible, he will come to understand that first you must believe in the salvation offered by Jesus alone and that you have to grow in holiness because nothing unholy will enter Heaven (Rev ch21). The Catholic Church offers a way to grow in holiness. Protestant faith traditions offer the free salvation won for us by Jesus. They generally fail to teach that you have to grow in holiness because you are either predestined for Heaven (as taught by John Calvin) or can only lose your salvation by denying Christ (as taught by Martin Luther). Jesus taught that we had to keep the 10 Commandments (Matthew 16 and Luke 18) and avoid the sins Paul lists in 1 Corinthians chapter 6 and Galatians chapter 5, to have eternal life. Jesus also requires us to do the works of

47

mercy laid out for us in the Bible. Failure to do the Works of Mercy (Matt ch5) will keep you out of Heaven (Matthew ch7&25) Teaching Salvation by Faith alone without Works afterward is risky business.

Salvation Through Faith and Works

Catholic Christians and Protestant Christians both agree that we are saved by God's Grace alone through Faith in Jesus Christ alone and that previous good works have nothing to do with our initial Salvation. There is only one Work that must be done to be saved. That is to accept, by God's Grace, the gift of Faith in Jesus' atoning death and resurrection for our sins.

What Protestants and Catholics don't agree on is what Works done after initial Salvation have to do with our final Salvation. The Catholic Church teaches that good works are necessary for salvation as members of the Body of Christ His Church. This is shown in Ephesians chapter 2:8-10 where it says we are saved by God's Grace, through Faith in Jesus Christ unto the Works God has laid out for us to do.

Protestants point to Romans chapter 3, Galatians chapter 2 and Ephesians chapter 2 to show that Paul taught that we are saved by Grace or Faith alone and not by Works. The key to understanding these chapters is to know the people Paul was preaching to. In the early Church there were some Jews that taught that new Gentile Christians still had to keep the Jewish ceremonial and food laws. These were known as the "Works of the Law". The Council of Jerusalem in Acts chapter 15 gave a decree that these laws no longer applied, but some Jews continued to insist that they be kept. The Dead Sea Scrolls, written 200 years before Jesus, have a scroll about the "works of the law", just as Paul referred to them. Paul is preaching to the Churches in Rome, Galatia and Ephesus to tell the Jewish Christians and the Gentile Christians that they are not saved by keeping the Jewish ceremonial and kosher laws because we are under the new Covenant in Jesus Christ.

Some Protestants teach that good works are a natural product of our initial salvation and show the sanctification of the Christian. Other Protestants teach that good works are a way to demonstrate that you are a Christian but contribute nothing to final salvation. Other Protestants teach that no works are necessary after initial salvation because it would be an insult to try to add to Jesus' finished work on the cross. Other Protestants teach that it doesn't matter if you do good works or sin after initial salvation because your salvation is guaranteed.

Many Protestants use the thief on the cross as an example of a person saved by Faith without Works. However, the thief on the cross did many works in the process of his salvation. He admonished his fellow sinner when he told him to be quiet because they were only getting what their sins deserved. He recognized Jesus as his Lord and Savior and asked Jesus to remember him when He came into His Kingdom. These two actions gave witness to Jesus mission to save us from our sins. This shows that even the thief on the cross did works after he came to Faith in Jesus. If a person dies right after coming to Faith they are still saved, but if you continue to live after coming to Faith in Jesus, He requires us to do more.

The Catholic Church teaches that after the initial work of salvation, future works are also required following what Paul taught in Ephesians 2:8-10. This is because Baptism incorporates us into the Body of Christ, His Church (1 Cor ch12). The works we do in the Body of Christ are for God's glory not ours. As we continue doing the works God has laid out for us to do, we become more like Jesus every day. Jesus tells us in Luke chapter 9 to take up our cross daily.

Paul tells us in Colossians 1:24 "I am now rejoicing in my sufferings for your sake, and in my flesh, I am completing what is lacking in Christ's afflictions for the sake of his body, that is, the church". This shows how we can suffer along with Christ for the sake of His Church. When we come to Christ, and are incorporated into His Body the Church through Baptism, we have to live like Christ every day. There is no limit on the number of good works we can do for God's glory. Galatians chapter 5 tells us that circumcision (work of the law) doesn't save us, but faith working through love does. Romans chapter 2 tells us that God will render to every man according to his works and that it is not the hearers of the law that are justified but the doers of the law who will be justified. In Philippians chapter 2 Paul tells us to work out your salvation with fear and trembling. For God is the one who works in you to both desire and to live the commandments to have eternal life. Paul tells us in 1 Corinthians that Jesus death and resurrection are both necessary for our salvation, so it is not Jesus' death alone that saves us. James chapter 2 tells us three times that Faith and Works are both necessary. In Matthew chapter 24 Jesus tells us that he who continues working in the Body of Christ to the end, shall be saved.

All of this comes together when we look at the Final
Judgment in Matthew chapter 7 where Jesus says "'Not
everyone who says to me, 'Lord, Lord', shall enter the
Kingdom of Heaven, but he who does the will of my
Father who is in Heaven". In Matthew chapter 25, Jesus
tells us that believers will be sorted out by the ones who
did and did not do the Works that Jesus told us we must
do in Matthew chapter 5. Romans chapter 2 tells us that
it is Not the hearers of the law that will be saved but the
Doers of the law that will be saved. In Luke chapters 12
and 14 we are told that we will be judged by what we did
not by what we knew. Revelation chapters 3, 14, 20 and
22 all tell us we will be judged by our Works and not by
Faith alone.

Can a Saved Person Lose Their Salvation?

Catholic Christians and Protestant Christians both agree
that we are saved by God's Grace through Faith in Jesus
Christ. Protestants and Catholics also agree that good
works are good evidence of being in a saved condition
(Eph2:8-10). However, there is disagreement on whether
a saved person can lose their salvation. The Catholic
Church and some Protestant churches teach that a saved
person can become unsaved if they commit certain really
bad sins. Other Protestant churches teach that all sins are
covered by Jesus so you can't lose your salvation.

Some Protestants, following the teachings of Martin
Luther and John Calvin, claim that you can't lose your
salvation,
because we do not have Free Will. Martin Luther taught
that either God or the devil will control your life. John
Calvin taught that God predestines some people for

Heaven and most people for Hell. These Protestants point to several passages in the Bible that seem to ensure Eternal Salvation for the truly saved.

John 3:16 "For God so loved the world, that He gave His only begotten Son, that whoever believes in Him shall not perish, but have eternal life."
John 6:39 "This is the will of Him who sent Me, that of all that He has given Me I lose nothing, but raise it up on the last day."
John 10:28-29 "I give eternal life to them, and they will never perish; and no one will snatch them out of My hand."
1 John 5:13" These things I have written to you who believe in the name of the Son of God, so that you may know that you have eternal life."
Romans 8:38-39 "For I am convinced that neither death, nor life, nor angels, nor principalities, nor present things, nor future things, nor powers, nor height, nor depth, nor any other creature will be able to separate us from the love of God in Christ Jesus our Lord."
Ephesians 1:13-14 "In Him, you also, after listening to the message of truth, the gospel of your salvation--having also believed, you were sealed in Him with the Holy Spirit of promise,"
Ephesians 4:30 "Do not grieve the Holy Spirit of God, by whom you were sealed for the day of redemption."
Hebrews 13:5 "Make sure that your character is free from the love of money, for He Himself has said, "I will never desert you, nor will I ever forsake you,"

All of these verses must be understood that they apply to those that continue in the Faith and are still members of the Body of Christ, His Church. For 'Once Saved Always Saved' Protestants there is no way to lose your salvation if you are one of God's 'elect' and predestined for Heaven as taught by John Calvin. Or all sins are 'covered' by Jesus' shed blood or are like a dung hill covered in snow as taught by Martin Luther. An emotional conversion experience and good works are evidence that you are one of the 'elect'. If some later fall away or 'backslide' seriously, then they were never really 'saved' to begin with. There is no definite way to really know who will continue in the Faith and who will fall away and backslide.

Other Protestants follow the teachings of Jacob Arminius and John Wesley who taught that we do have Free Will to choose to follow God or not. They taught that God provides sufficient Grace to save us and draw us to Him, but we can reject that Grace. We can choose to leave God's Family at any time and turn back to our sinful ways. The Methodist church of John Wesley provided a way to grow in holiness by responding to God's Grace and go to Heaven. Protestant churches that follow this theology require their members to repent of their sins to have their salvation restored. Some require serious sin to be repented of in front of the Church Board. Others require their members to repent and confess their sins to God alone.

The Catholic Church teaches that some people are predestined to go to Heaven, but we don't have a method for determining who the 'elect' are. Instead the Catholic Church provides a way to have the original state of holiness of Adam and Eve restored to a person through Baptism.
This state of holiness is maintained through the sacrament of reconciliation (confession). We grow in holiness by receiving Grace in the Eucharist, Confirmation, reading the Bible and doing the good works that God has laid out for us to do (Eph 2:10).

The Catholic Church distinguishes between Mortal and Venial sins based on 1 John chapter 5. Mortal sins go against the 10 commandments and are done with full knowledge and consent of our will and must be confessed for forgiveness. Jesus taught that we had to keep the 10 Commandments in Matthew chapter 16 and Luke chapter 18 to have eternal life. Venial sins are lesser sins that can be washed away with Holy Water before Mass and receiving the Eucharist. All sin is an offense against God and should be avoided.

These verses show that we must continue living in the Body of Christ and avoid sin to maintain our salvation. Matthew 10:22 tells us that he who endures until the end shall be saved. So, we must continue to live in the Body of Christ to be saved not just at the beginning.
John3:16 tells us that "For God so loved the world that He gave His only begotten Son, so that everyone who believes in Him might not perish, but have eternal life." The key word here is "believe" which originally meant to continue to believe in and follow Jesus.
Hebrews 6:4-6 It is impossible for those who have once been enlightened, ... and who have fallen away, to be brought back to repentance. Hebrews 10:26 reminds us that if we sin deliberately there is no longer a sacrifice for our salvation and we can end up in Hell if we do not repent.
In 1 Corinthians chapter 6 Paul tells us of many sins that will keep us out of Heaven if left unrepentant.
In Galatians chapter 5 Paul again tells us of many sins that will keep us out of Heaven. In chapter 6 Paul tells us that we need avoid sin, live in the Spirit of Jesus and do good works.

In Philippians chapters 2, 3 and 4 Paul tell us we need to work out our own salvation with fear and trembling. He does not consider his own salvation secure but encourages others to continue to work with him so that their names will continue to be in the Book of Life. Revelation chapter 3 tells us that those that overcome the temptation of sin are written in the Book of Life. Revelation chapter 13 warns that those who worship the beast will not be in the Book of Life. Revelation chapter 20 tells us that the great and small will stand before the Great White Throne of Judgement and that those whose names are not in the Book of Life will be cast into Hell. Revelation chapter 21 tells us that those without the stain of sin and whose names are written in the Book of Life will enter Heaven.

In Luke chapter 15 we have the story of the prodigal son who took his inheritance (salvation) and left his father's house (the Church) and went off to live a life of sin (losing his salvation). When all appears lost to the son, he repents and returns to his father's house (the Church). His father calls for a feast in honor of his son returning to the household (the Church). The father explains to his other son that his brother who was dead in sin has returned to life in his father's house. The repentance of a sinner is the reason for the celebration on earth as it is in Heaven.

The Scripture is very clear "the soul that sins will surely die" (Ezekiel 18:20) without regard to the Church that they attend. The Apostle Paul makes it abundantly clear that those who don't repent of their sins will not enter the Kingdom of Heaven in 1 Corinthians chapter 6 and Galatians chapter 5. The Apostle John records in Revelation chapter 21 that those who are un-clean because of sin won't enter Heaven. Jesus tells us in

Matthew 7:21 Not everyone that says unto me, Lord, Lord, shall enter into the kingdom of Heaven. There is no way we can continue to sin and still go to Heaven without repentance.

Eternal Security is promised to us as long as we maintain our connection to Christ. Our Free Will allows us to walk away at any time and lose our salvation. We can restore our salvation through repentance, confession and penance. We have the opportunity to return to Jesus at any time up until death. However, we never know when we might lose our life in an instant and miss our chance to return to Jesus. This is why we need to always maintain our relationship with Jesus so we can have eternal life with Him.

How the Sacrament of Reconciliation Keeps Us Holy

Catholic Christians and Protestants Christians have different understandings on the effects of sin. Protestant Christians get their understanding from Martin Luther and John Calvin who taught imputed or declared righteousness. These early Protestants taught that we are "hidden" by Christ so God can't see our sins and once we are incorporated into God's family with no way to lose that. This new theology denies our free will which allows us to walk away from God's family like in the story of the Prodigal Son who later repented and returned to God's family (Luke ch15).

The Catholic Church follows the understanding of sin inherited from the Jews. When the Jews sinned, they would go to the Temple and confess their sins to the Priest there. After confessing they would offer something back to God in atonement for their sins. The Bible teaches that Baptism washes all previous sin away (Acts ch2 and 22). Baptism incorporates us into the Body of Christ (1Cor ch12) and we become actually Holy like Jesus. If you sin after Baptism you must confess your sin and do something to restore your relationship with Jesus and the Church.

In the book of Leviticus chapter 19 we learn how the Jews had to reconcile sins by confessing to a Priest who offered a sacrifice and acted as a mediator for the repentant sinner. In 2 Samuel chapters 11 and 12 we find the story of David, Bathsheba, Uriah and the Prophet Nathan. David commits adultery with Bathsheba, Uriah's wife, and then has Uriah killed in battle. The Prophet Nathan confronts David and he confesses his sin to Nathan. Nathan tells David that God has put away his sin, but for his punishment, the child he created with Bathsheba while she was still married to Uriah will die. This shows that there is always something that must be done in reparation for sin even after forgiveness. David offers a perfect act of contrition in 2 Samuel chapter 12 that can reconcile a person with God. The Sacrament of Reconciliation offers guaranteed forgiveness without perfect contrition through the authority of Jesus given to the Apostles and passed down to the Bishops and Priests (John ch20, 1 Tim ch2).

In Matthew chapter 9, Jesus tells us that He was given authority on earth to forgive sins (a power reserved to God alone) and proves it with miraculous healings and then Scripture notes this same authority was given to "men" (plural). Jesus makes it clear He intended to give His authority to men. In John chapter 20, right after His Resurrection, Jesus gives this awesome power to his Apostles with the words: "Receive the Holy Spirit. If you forgive the sins of any, they are forgiven; if you retain the sins of any, they are retained." They cannot grant forgiveness of sins if they don't know the sins just like the Jewish Temple Priests. This authority comes through the gift of the Holy Spirit. This authority is given by Jesus to Peter and then the other Apostles in Matthew chapter 16 when He gives them the authority to bind and loose. This includes sins. Jesus allowed for us to receive spiritual consolation and counsel in this beautiful Sacrament through His authorized ministers. We also see this in what is called the Sacrament of anointing the sick. James chapter 5 tells how someone can be healed through anointing with oil and confessing their sins to another person. James does not say confess your sins straight to God but instead they are to go to the "elders" (Acts 14:23; 15:2).

Catholics follow the Bible and distinguish between Mortal and Venial sins based on 1 John chapter 5. Mortal sins are those that go against the 10 commandments and are done with full knowledge and consent of our will. They must be confessed for forgiveness. Venial sins are lesser sins that can be washed away with Holy Water before Mass, receiving the Eucharist, reading the Bible and other good works. If a venial sin is repeated often, it can rise to a mortal sin and should be confessed to break the habit through the Grace given through the sacrament. All sin is an offense against God and should be avoided.

Paul writes in 2 Corinthians 5:18-20, "And all things are of God, who has reconciled us to himself by Jesus Christ, and has given to us the ministry of reconciliation; This shows that God was in Christ, reconciling the world unto Himself, not imputing their trespasses on them; and has committed to us the words of reconciliation. Now then we (the Apostles and the Bishops they ordained) are ambassadors for Christ, as though God did beseech you by us: we pray for you on the behalf of Christ so that you can be reconciled to God. "

Baptism brings us into the family of God. When we sin, God does not kick us out. Instead, using our Free Will, we are like the prodigal son (Luke ch15) who walks away from God's family. When we repent, the Sacrament of Reconciliation is the feast the Father throws welcoming us back to the family of God. The Catholic Church does recognize that some of us are predestined for Heaven but does not specify a way to identify them. Baptism incorporates us into the Body of Christ. When we sin, it affects the Body of Christ like an infection. When we confess our sins, Jesus forgives our sins, through the Priest, which is like putting a Band-aid on our sin and He remembers it no more. Our penance is the healing process that restores our relationship and holiness as members of the Body of Christ because nothing un-clean can enter Heaven (Rev ch21).

Jesus taught that we had to keep the 10 Commandments in Matthew chapter 16 and Luke chapter 18 to have eternal life.

In 1 Corinthians chapter 6 Paul writes, "Do you not know that wrongdoers will not inherit the kingdom of God? Do not be deceived! Fornicators, idolaters, adulterers, male prostitutes, sodomites, thieves, the greedy, drunkards, revilers, robbers—none of these will inherit the kingdom of God. And this is what some of you used to be. But you were washed, you were sanctified, you were justified in the name of the Lord Jesus Christ and in the Spirit of our God." In Galatians chapter 5 Paul writes "Now the works of the flesh are obvious: immorality, impurity, licentiousness, idolatry, sorcery, hatreds, rivalry, jealousy, outbursts of fury, acts of selfishness, dissensions, factions, occasions of envy-drinking bouts, orgies, and the like. I warn you, as I warned you before, that those who do such things will not inherit the kingdom of God." This shows that we need to lead Holy lives to go to Heaven or at least have our Holiness restored through confession.

In Hebrews chapter 6 we learn that if Christians who come to Faith in Jesus fall away (sin) they can be renewed again through repentance. In Hebrews 13:17 it says "Obey them that have the rule over you, and submit yourselves: for they watch for your souls, as they that must give account, that they may do it with joy, and not with grief: for that is unprofitable for you." In 1Timothy 1:6 and 4:14, Paul reminds Timothy that the office of bishop had been conferred on him through the laying on of hands.

Jesus is the only one who can forgive sins, but He delegated that authority to His Apostles who passed it on to the Bishops they ordained. During the Sacrament of Reconciliation (confession) we hear the words of absolution from Jesus through the Priest. The priests are ordained by the laying of hands all the way back to the Apostles.

The New Testament Christians didn't offer something to be burned at the Temple, but they were required to confess their sins and do penance. The Sacrament of Reconciliation is the original practice of Christians from the beginning of the Church that Jesus left behind when He ascended into Heaven. Catholics are obligated to confess all mortal sins at least once a year. Many find it a good practice to go to confession once a month. Priests are always happy to welcome back a person who has not been to confession for many years. You are only required to confess the sin and number of times. Details are not necessary. The Catechism of the Catholic Church covers Reconciliation in sections 1422 through 1470.

The Didache, which is the Teaching of the 12 Apostles, from 70AD requires the early Christians to "confess your sins in church, and do not go up to your prayer with an evil conscience. On the Lord's Day...break bread...after confessing your transgressions so that your sacrifice may be pure"

In 74AD in the Epistle of Barnabas, he writes, "You shall confess your sins. You shall not go to prayer with an evil conscience."
In 107AD Ignatius of Antioch writes to the Philadelphians, "To all them that repent, the Lord grants forgiveness, if they turn in penitence to the unity of God, and to communion with the Bishop"

In 115AD Polycarp writes to the Philippians "And let the Presbyters (Priests) be compassionate and merciful to all, bringing back those that wander (sinners)".

In 215AD Hippolytus of Rome writes, "The bishop conducting the ordination of the new bishop shall pray to offer to you the gifts of your Holy Church, and by the Spirit of the high priesthood to have the authority to forgive sins, in accord with your command".

Purgatory is in the Bible

Using the Bible and reason, Christians have developed many doctrines like the Trinity. Many Protestants ask,

"Where is Purgatory in the Bible?" Purgatory is a doctrine that can be reasoned to by using many verses in the Bible just like the Trinity. All Christians believe that Jesus' death on the cross provided all the Grace to save everyone and to allow us to become Holy, so we can enter Heaven. Purgatory is the place or process of finishing that transformation from a state of still being attached to minor sins to being fully sanctified and ready to enter Heaven. Few of us take full advantage of the Grace offered by Jesus to make us Holy here on earth, so most of us will need a final clean up before entering Heaven.

Starting with the Jewish understanding of forgiving sins, animals were offered to reconcile the Israelites with God in the Book of Leviticus chapter 5. The animals were offered, as a gift back to God in atonement for sin, not for God to punish instead of the sinning Israelites. In 2 Samuel chapter 12, after Nathan tells David that God has forgiven his sin with Bathsheba, he tells David his son will die. This confirms that something must be done to reconcile us to God even after forgiveness. The Jews prayed for the sins of their dead in 2 Maccabees chapter 12 and still offer prayers for their dead today. For these prayers to have any effect there must be a place after death where sins can be forgiven.

Christ's death on the cross is the final sacrifice that provides all the Grace needed to atone for all sins against God. It also provides the Grace for us to be sanctified which allows us to become Holy and enter Heaven. When a person is baptized, all previous sin is washed away (Acts ch 2&22) and we are incorporated into the Body of Christ (1 Cor ch12).

In 1 John chapter 5 we learn that there are some sins unto death (mortal sins) and some sins not unto death (venial sins). If we die with unconfessed mortal sins on our soul we will not be welcomed into Heaven. If we die while still committing venial sins, we can still be admitted to Heaven after atoning for these sins in what we call Purgatory. All sins are an offense to God and should be avoided.

In Matthew chapter 21 Jesus says that blasphemy against the Holy Spirit cannot be forgiven in this life or the next, which implies some sins can be forgiven in the next life.

Purgatory provides a place or process for us to finish our penance for any sins committed after Baptism before entering Heaven. In Revelation chapter 21 we learn that nothing unclean can enter Heaven. Since few of us reach full sanctification here on Earth there must be a way to finish sanctification on the way to Heaven.

Many Protestants point to when Jesus says, "It is finished" on the cross in John chapter 19 to show that there is nothing we need to do for our salvation. Here Jesus is referring to the New Testament Passover that He started in the upper room being finished because He had just drunk the wine finishing that Passover meal with the fourth cup of wine. Some people are still living with Luther's misunderstanding that Jesus' sacrifice covers our sins like snow over a dung heap. If that is their understanding, then all those sins still need to be reconciled before entering Heaven. That can happen in Purgatory too. God knows our sins. We cannot "hide" behind Jesus.

In 1 Corinthians chapter 3, Paul writes, "If the work stands that someone built upon the foundation (Jesus), that person will receive a wage. But if someone's work is burned up, that one will suffer loss; the person will be saved, but only as through fire. This may be the refining fire of Purgatory.

In 2 Corinthians chapter 5 Paul writes, "So we are always confident, knowing that while we are at **home in the body, we are absent from the Lord**. For we walk by faith, not by sight. We are confident, yes, **well pleased rather to be absent from the body and to be present with the Lord**". This does not say that we are instantly present with the Lord when we are separated from our bodies. It says that we would be "pleased to be absent from the body and present with the Lord". When we compare these verses to 1 Corinthians 15:51–54 it becomes even clearer, "Behold, I tell you a mystery: We shall not all sleep, but we shall all be changed— in a moment, in the twinkling of an eye, at the last trumpet. For the trumpet will sound, and the dead will be raised incorruptible, and we shall be changed. For this corruptible must put on incorruption, and this mortal must put on immortality. "Death is swallowed up in victory." This tells us that at death, we are all going to be changed. At the last trumpet, which is the second coming of Jesus, all people still living will be changed quickly but they will still be changed. In 2 Timothy chapter 1 we find Paul praying for his dead friend Onesiphorus. Paul prays for his friend's soul that he may be with God in Heaven. Paul must have had some hope that his prayers were effective.

In Hebrews chapter 12 Paul writes, "Now, you have approached Mount Zion and the city of the living God, the heavenly Jerusalem, and countless angels in festal gathering, and the assembly of the firstborn enrolled in heaven, and God the judge of all, and the spirits of the just who have been made perfect." This Heavenly Jerusalem that we may go to when we die to be with God, Jesus and the angels, has spirits who are perfect. Since few of us die in a state of perfection there has to be a change in us to be made perfect so we can be with the angels in Heaven until Jesus' second coming. From this we learn that at death, or the second coming of Jesus (1Thess ch4), we shall be changed from corruptible (capable of sinning) to incorruptible (incapable of sinning), so we can enter Heaven because nothing unclean can enter there (Rev ch21).

Many of the early Christians had writings on their coffins asking that people pray for them after they died. Catholics continue the practice of praying for the dead to ask God to speed our friend's transformation from sinners to Saints. Praying for the dead in Hell can't help them. Praying for the dead in Heaven is unnecessary, so there must be some state of being between life on earth and life in Heaven. We call that place Purgatory.

Augustine on Purgatory and Prayers for the Dead 400AD. It is not to be doubted that the dead are aided by prayers of the Holy Church, and by the salutary sacrifice (Mass), and by the alms, which are offered for their spirits. For this, which has been handed down by the Fathers, the universal church observes. The man who perhaps has not cultivated the land and has allowed it to be overrun with brambles has in this life the curse of his land on all his works, and after this life he will have either purgatorial fire or eternal punishment. As also, after the resurrection, there will be some of the dead to whom, after they have endured the pains proper to the spirits of the dead, mercy shall be accorded, and acquittal from the punishment of the eternal fire. For were there not some whose sins, though not remitted in this life, shall be remitted in that which is to come, it could not be truly said, "They shall not be forgiven, neither in this world, neither in that which is to come."

Pope Paul VI: "It is a divinely revealed truth that sins bring punishments inflicted by God's sanctity and justice. These must be expiated either on this earth through the sorrows, miseries and calamities of this life and above all through death, **OR** else in the life beyond through fire and torments or "purifying" punishments." (Pope Paul VI, Indulgentarum Doctrina, 2)

Pope Urban V: "We ask if you have believed and now believe that there is a purgatory to which depart the souls of those dying in grace **who have not yet made complete satisfaction for their sins**. Also, if you have believed and now believe that they will be tortured by fire for a time and that as soon as they are cleansed, even before the day of judgment, they may come to the true and eternal beatitude which consists in the vision of God face to face and in love." (Pope Urban V, Super Quibusdam).

Indulgences

Indulgences offer an opportunity to have all previous penance for sins to be completed at the time the indulgence is granted. It is not a get out of sin free card. The Catholic Church teaches that when we are Baptized all previous sin is washed away (Act 2 and 22) and we are saved (1 Peter ch3). All sins after baptism have to be reconciled through repentance, confession and penance.

We become members of the Body of Christ through Baptism (1 Cor ch12) and as members of the Body of Christ we can help each other with the penance that must be done to heal our offense against God when we sin. Since one member of a family can help another with a task, a fellow Christian can also help a fellow Christian with their penance.

Indulgences can be gained by doing a certain work or action for yourself or a loved one. To gain an indulgence you must be in a state of Grace by having all previous sin absolved or removed through the sacrament of reconciliation or confession. You must also receive the Eucharist at Mass and pray for the intentions of the Pope.

The practice of indulgences goes back to at least the 200s in Christianity. Before Christianity became a tolerated religion in 311AD, Christians were being severely persecuted on and off by the Romans. When some people sacrificed to the Roman Emperor to save their life, they were expelled from communion with the Church until they did a penance which could last for years. Some of these penitents appealed to Christians that were waiting for execution in prison because they refused to sacrifice to the Emperor. The person doing penance sometimes asked the person in prison to ask the local Bishop to have their penance reduced through the sacrifice of the person in prison. The thought was that the merit of Grace of the condemned prisoners could be given to the penitents that were still free. The local Bishops were not quick to let these penitents off easy, but with the understanding that we are all members of the Body of Christ, one member can help another member with their penance.

In 115AD Polycarp of Smyrna, who learned the Faith from the Apostle John, wrote a cover letter for the letters of Ignatius of Antioch that he was forwarding to the Church in Philippi. Polycarp writes that alms atone for sins which is a reference to a verse in the book of Tobit chapter 4. This is where the Church gets its teaching that alms for the poor can be offered as penance for sins.

The Catholic Church teaches that the excess Grace, merited by other members of the Body of Christ, His Church, can be offered to those who are not yet in Heaven because nothing unclean can enter there. This helps them to become fully sanctified and worthy of entry into Heaven. Just as we can help each other do things on Earth, the Saints in Heaven can help sanctify us here on Earth. All of this only makes sense when you think of us as members of the Body of Christ (1 Cor ch12) that can help each other, and that we must be Holy before we can enter Heaven (Rev ch21).

Indulgences are covered in the Catechism in paragraphs 1471-1479. A person can gain a partial or plenary (full) indulgence for many different acts. The Indulgence can be applied to yourself or to someone in Purgatory.

Apostolic Authority, Succession and Tradition

The Disciples that became the Apostles handed on what Jesus taught them to the new Christians. Some of what they taught was written down. Since parchment was expensive and few people could read, the Faith was passed on orally more than by writing. The Oral Tradition was later supported by the Written Tradition.

Jesus left behind a Church with Kingdom like Authority because the Messiah was to sit on the Throne of David. The Kings of that time had ministers that helped run the Kingdom. Their authority was symbolized by their Keys. Jesus gave the "Keys" to Peter and the Apostles (Matt ch16) who handed on their authority through Apostolic Succession. In Luke chapter 17 Jesus tells His Disciples "He who hears you hears Me and he who rejects you rejects Me and the One who sent me." The Disciples who became the Apostles had the Authority from God through Jesus.

In John chapter 20 right after Jesus' resurrection, He tells the Apostles that any sins they forgive are forgiven and any sins that are retained are retained. This is a passing on of Jesus' Authority from the Father to His Apostles.

In Matthew chapter 28, before ascending into Heaven, Jesus tells the Apostles that all the authority that God gave Him, He passes onto the Apostles. Jesus also told the Apostles to go out and teach the world everything that He taught and to Baptize them in the name of the Father, Son and Holy Spirit. Jesus promises to be with them until the end of the age.

In Acts chapter 1 the Apostles cast lots to fill the vacancy that Judas left. Peter says, "Let another take his office" (Psalm 109). This shows that from the beginning the Apostles recognized they held an office that would have successors.

When the Apostles went out and founded Churches, they would appoint successors that we now call Bishops by laying hands on them. This handing down of authority is called Apostolic Succession. The line of authority is from God the Father to Jesus; Jesus to the Apostles; the

Apostles to the Bishops they ordained; and the Bishops to the Bishops that they ordained.

When there were disputes on doctrine, the Bishops held Councils (local synods and worldwide ecumenical) to work them out. The Bishops continue to hold Councils that give Holy Spirit inspired, binding, decrees to the Christians like the Church leaders in Acts chapter 15 at the Council of Jerusalem. The decree of the Council of Jerusalem directly contradicted Genesis chapter 17 where God required Abraham and his descendants to be circumcised. This shows that the Apostles had the Authority from God to change the law of the Old Covenant.

In 1 Timothy chapter 4, Paul tells Timothy to be a good minister, to teach soundly and to not neglect the gift he was given through the laying on of his hands. Paul reminds him again in 2 Timothy 1:6 "Remember the gift you received with the laying on of my hands" referring to when he made Timothy a Bishop. Paul also warns Timothy to be careful about whom he lays hands on and be sure they know and follow the Faith before laying hands on them. This shows how the Faith was passed on through the teachers not just a book. In Ephesians chapter 4 Paul also lists the different positions in the Church like Prophets, teachers, readers etc. In Titus chapter 1, Paul reminds Titus that he left him in Crete to teach the people rightly and appoint presbyters (Priests/Bishops) in every town to properly hand on the Faith. Paul also tells Titus that the men he appoints should teach and appoint other men following the Tradition of Apostolic Succession.

In 1 Timothy chapter 3 Paul tells Timothy that the Church is the Pillar and Foundation of the Truth, not the

Bible. John's Gospel chapters 20 and 21 also tells us that everything is not written in what we now call the Bible because no book could hold it all. In 2 Thessalonians chapter 2 Paul tells us to, "Hold fast to the Traditions I have taught you by word and by writing." In 1 Corinthians chapter 10 and 11, Paul tells the Corinthians of the Church practices and that we have no other practices and neither do the Churches of God. Unity in practice was expected among the Christians then and now. The Faith was passed on through Apostolic Tradition as well as the later Apostolic writings that became the New Testament.

It took about 350 years for the Catholic Church to decide which of the early Christian writings were the inspired Word of God based on the Apostolic origin of the writing, how well it supported the Apostolic Tradition and if it was read in the Churches known to be founded by Apostles.

Originally the scrolls that the Jews used had only the consonant letters on them to save space. The vowels used with the consonant letters were taught by the Rabbis to their students who would read it during the worship activity in the Synagogues. Later, vowel points were added between the lines of consonants to establish the full spelling of the words. The text of Jewish Scriptures with consonants and vowels is known as the Masoretic Text which was developed between 400 and 900AD.

The interpretation of the Old Testament was passed on by Oral Tradition of the Rabbis, in the same way the interpretation of the New Testament was passed on by the Apostles to the Bishops they ordained and onto the Bishops they ordained. When there were disputes about interpretation, they held local councils (synods) to determine interpretation of the scriptures.

The later Ecumenical Councils gave binding decrees just like the Council of Jerusalem (Acts ch15). The problem is that some people don't want to accept the authority of the Council and split. This happened in 431 after the Council of Ephesus and in 451 after the Council of Chalcedon. Some Christians always reject the decisions of Councils, even up through Vatican II, and put their Salvation at risk.

In 90AD the Church in Corinth had a dispute so they wrote a letter to the Bishop of Rome. Clement, Bishop of Rome, wrote back that the Apostles received their authority from Jesus and the Bishops received their authority from the Apostles. This shows that from the beginning the Bishops recognized their authority came from the Apostles.

In 107AD Ignatius Bishop of Antioch writes that the teachings of the Church are passed on through the Bishops not a book. Ignatius also tells us that wherever the Bishop is, there is the catholic Church.

In 180AD Irenaeus Bishop of Lyon wrote a 5-volume book against Heresies. Irenaeus learned the Faith from Polycarp Bishop of Smyrna, who learned the Faith from the Apostle John. Irenaeus writes that if two Churches have a doctrinal dispute, they need to see which Church can trace its history back to an Apostle. Or he says, "All you need to do is find out what the Church in Rome teaches, because all Churches must agree with that Church because Peter and Paul taught there."

In our modern American society few people want to accept authority, especially when it comes to interpretation of the Bible or religion in general. People want to believe what they are convinced is right. Unity can only be maintained through Authority. The question is whose authority do you accept? Our best chance of Salvation is through the Church that Jesus left behind to carry on His Mission. That Church is the Catholic Church.

Pope or Bishop of Rome

The Pope is the visible head of the Church that Jesus left behind after He ascended into Heaven. Most Christians know that Jesus said "You are Peter and, on this Rock, I will build my Church" It is in Matthews Gospel chapter 16 verse 18. Catholics see this as Jesus ordaining Peter as the first Pope, but Protestants say that Jesus was talking about Peter's Faith not his Office.

This passage needs to be understood in the larger context of the chapter. In Matthew 16:17 Jesus tells Peter "Blessed are you Simon son of Jonah" which is clearly a blessing. In verse 19 Jesus gives Peter the Keys to the Kingdom and the authority to bind and loose. This is another gift from Jesus. It is therefore logical to recognize that verse 18 is also a blessing when Simon has his name changed to Peter. This blessing shows that Peter is the Rock that Jesus will build His Church on, not just Peter's confession of Faith. Verses 17, 18 and 19 all apply to Peter. Jesus does not apply 17 to Peter, 18 to Himself and 19 to Peter again. Jesus also promises in verse 20 that the "Gates of Hell will not prevail against it". If the Church that Jesus founded on Peter has been corrupted, then Jesus did not protect it as He promised.

Protestants argue that the Greek word "Petra" for little rock is used for "Peter" and the Greek word for big rock "Petros" refers to Peter's Faith in Jesus, so this means that Jesus wasn't talking about Peter personally. The New Testament was written in Greek but Jesus spoke Aramaic and the same word Kepha is used for big and little rock. Therefore, Jesus was really talking about Peter both times. Some people will question Peter's mistaken grasp at authority in verse 22 where Peter tries to keep Jesus from going to Jerusalem to be crucified. Peter later denies knowing Jesus 3 times as Jesus predicted. After Jesus' resurrection, Jesus restores Peter in his office in John chapter 21 verses 15-17. Here Jesus asks Peter 3 times "Do you Love Me" to restore Peter's denials. Jesus also tells Peter to feed my lambs, tend my sheep, and feed my sheep. These commands are given to Peter not the 10 other disciples and indicate that Peter is to teach new believers, take care of the 10 other Disciples, and to teach the other Disciples.

Peter's primacy is quite obvious in the New Testament. Peter is mentioned by name more than 100 times. John is second at 29 times. Peter is always listed at the beginning of the list of Apostles or as the leader of the Apostles even though Andrew was the first Apostle called by Jesus. In the Book of Acts chapter 1 Peter tells the other Apostles that we have to replace Judas. In chapter 2 Peter preaches and converts the Jews. He tells them to repent and be Baptized to forgive their sins. Peter heals the crippled man. Peter gives out the discipline that kills Ananias and Sapphira for lying to the Holy Spirit and the Church. Peter heals Lydia and Tabitha. Peter receives the vision that it is OK to eat all foods. Peter is the one called to convert Cornelius the first Gentile and his family to Christianity. In Acts chapter 15 there is a dispute about

Gentiles needing to become Jews before becoming Christians. Peter gives the final testimony about Cornelius receiving the Holy Spirit without becoming a Jew, so Gentiles don't need to be circumcised. There is no other discussion after Peter's testimony and the Jerusalem Council issues a binding decree that Gentiles can be brought into the Church without having to keep the Jewish works of the law.

After Paul's conversion, he goes to Jerusalem to learn the Faith from Peter and James (Acts ch21). Later Paul rebukes someone named Cephas for not eating with the Gentiles in Antioch (Gal ch2). Some consider this Cephas as the Apostle Peter, but Eusebius the early Church historian explains that this Cephas is another person. Even if it is the Apostle Peter, it only shows that the Pope does not always act correctly even though he has the authority to teach infallibly. The Jews continued to recognize the Chair of Moses where they received authoritative teaching. Jesus told the disciples that they should do what the Scribes and Pharisees teach from the Chair of Moses, but do not copy what they do. The Pope teaches from the Chair of Peter. We need to follow what the Church teaches but not the bad example of clergy and fellow Christians.

When the Jewish disciples heard Jesus tell Peter that He was giving him the Keys to the Kingdom, they recognized the authority of a minister from the dynasty of King David. Jesus is the Messiah that sits on the Throne of David. In Isaiah chapter 22 we learn that a successor of King David named Hezekiah, had a minister named Shebna who is replaced by Eliakim. The authority of the office is shown by the robe he wears and Key he carries. Keys at this time were large so they could reach through thick walls to operate the lock mechanism inside. When

Jesus tells Peter that He is giving him the Keys to the Kingdom, Peter and the Disciples knew that Peter would have similar authority. Peter was to become the Prime Minister over the whole Church and the rest of the Disciples would become Ministers in their own areas with authority to bind and loose. The Disciples also recognized the office was handed on to successors as it was in the Kingdom of David. The Book of Revelation chapter 3 verse 7 uses similar symbolism, plainly showing Jesus having the key of David in His Kingdom in Heaven. Jesus left Peter behind on earth so that we would have a representative to guide the Church that Jesus founded. That office was passed on to successors like the other Apostles passed on their offices to the Bishops they ordained.

In 90AD, the Church at Corinth had a dispute and wrote the Bishop of Rome for clarification. Pope St. Clement, Bishop of Rome, writes a letter to the Corinthians to resolve the problem. The Corinthians may have written to the Church in the destroyed Jerusalem, or the Church in Antioch, or to the Apostle John, but they received a letter from Clement of Rome and it was read in their Church and others at a yearly festival to commemorate the occasion.

In 107AD Ignatius of Antioch writes to the Church in Rome that he does not command them like Peter and Paul did. Ignatius writes that the Church in Rome presides over Christianity and to not try and save him when he gets there.

In 115AD Polycarp of Smyrna goes to visit the Bishop of Rome about the dating of Easter. Polycarp didn't go to Jerusalem or any other early Christian city because he knew where the authority was.

In 180AD Irenaeus writes in his book Against Heresies that all Churches must be in communion with the Church of Rome because of its preeminence since Peter and Paul taught there.

In 200AD Tertullian in his Prescription against Heresies writes that there is an authoritative throne of the teaching
of the Apostles in Rome. There are many later references to the Primacy of the Bishop of Rome.

The Protestant reformers developed their own interpretation of the Bible to base their new churches on. There are now thousands and thousands of Protestant denominations with a large variety of interpretations of the Bible based on their founders interpretation. The Bible Alone does not provide unity.

The Orthodox Churches share much in common with the Catholic Church, but they rely on the decisions of Councils to maintain their unity. However, some churches have broken away from the original Catholic Church when they disagreed with the decisions of the Ecumenical Councils of Ephesus in 531 and Chalcedon in 451. Councils and the Bible have not been able to maintain the Unity that Jesus desired

The Catholic Church consists of the Roman/Latin Rite and Eastern Rite Churches. They use the Bible that they assembled, the decisions of Councils and the guidance of the Pope to determine doctrine which has maintained unity for the last 2000 years. There are 22 different Eastern Rite Catholic Churches that are in union with the Bishop of Rome. They often use the liturgy of St. James and hold the same doctrines as the Roman Catholic

Church. The liturgy of the Eastern Rite Churches is similar to the Roman liturgy and is said in the language appropriate for that Rite.

The Catechism describes the Office of the Pope in paragraphs 880 through 887.

One, Holy, Catholic and Apostolic Church
The Four Marks of the Church

In the Nicene Creed, we profess, "We believe in One, Holy, Catholic, and Apostolic Church": these are the four marks of the Church.

Before Jesus ascended into Heaven, He prayed that we would all be one like He and the Father are One (John ch17). The Church is one in three ways: first its source is the Holy Trinity, a perfect unity of three divine persons — Father, Son, and Holy Spirit; second its founder, Jesus Christ, who came to reconcile all mankind through His death and resurrection; and third, because of its "soul," the Holy Spirit, who dwells in the souls of the faithful, who unites all of the faithful into one communion of believers, and who guides the Church. The "oneness" of the Catholic Church is also visible through our Creed and our other teachings, the celebration of the sacraments, and the hierarchical structure based on the apostolic succession preserved and handed on through the Sacrament of Holy Orders. In our oneness, we find diversity, because we are all Baptized into the Body of Christ (1 Cor ch12) and therefore members of the Body of Christ, His Church. We all have our part to play in bringing Jesus to the World through our lives while cooperating with the other members of the Body of Christ.

The Church is also Holy by our Baptism into the Body of Christ, His Church. Therefore, our sins not only affect us but the Whole Church. Jesus is the source of all holiness. Jesus is the One mediator and the way of salvation and is present to us in His body which is the Church. Christ makes the Church Holy through Him, the Church provides a path to Holiness. Through the ministry of the Church and the power of the Holy Spirit, Jesus provides many sources of Grace, especially through the sacraments. Therefore, through its teaching, prayer, worship, and good works, the Church is a visible sign of holiness. As members of the Church, we are called to holiness. Every Catholic must therefore aim at Christian perfection and play his part, in the Church. The Church has many outstanding examples of holiness in the lives of the saints of every age. No matter how dark the times of our Church past, present or future, there are always great saints through whom the light of Christ radiates.

The Church is also catholic. Around 107AD St. Ignatius of Antioch used this word meaning "universal" to describe the Church (Letter to the Smyrnaens). The Church is Catholic in that Christ is universally present in the Church and that He has commissioned the Church to evangelize the world. In Matthew 28:19 right before Jesus ascended in to Heaven it says, "Go therefore and make disciples of all the nations". The Church here on earth is called the Church militant and is united to the Church triumphant in Heaven and the Church suffering in Purgatory.

The Church is apostolic because Jesus gave His authority to His apostles, the first bishops. He entrusted a special authority to St. Peter, the first Pope and Bishop of Rome, to act as His representative here on earth. This authority has been handed down through the Sacrament of Holy Orders in what we call apostolic succession from Bishop to Bishop, and then by extension to Priests and Deacons. No Bishop, Priest, or Deacon in the Catholic Church is self-ordained. The Holy Spirit calls men to serve in ministry. They are taught by the Church and serve through the authority given to them by other Bishops in union with the Pope. The Church is also apostolic in that the deposit of faith found in both Sacred Scripture and Sacred Tradition was preserved, taught, and handed on by the apostles.

Under the guidance of the Holy Spirit, the Bishops and Priests have the duty to preserve, teach, defend, and hand on the deposit of faith. The Holy Spirit protects the Church from teaching error because Jesus promised to be with His Church until the end of the Age (Matt ch28). The Magisterium of the Church addresses current issues, such as nuclear war, euthanasia, in vitro fertilization, protected by the guidance of the Holy Spirit as Jesus promised.

These four marks of the Church one, holy, catholic, and apostolic are fully present in the Catholic Church. Other Christian churches accept and profess the Creed, and possess elements of truth and sanctification, but only the Catholic Church has the fullness of these marks.

The Second Vatican Council taught, "This Church (which Christ founded), constituted and organized as a society in the present world, subsists in the Catholic Church, which is governed by the successor of Peter and by the bishops in communion with him" (Dogmatic Constitution on the Church, #8), and "For it is through Christ's Catholic

Church alone, which is the universal help towards salvation, that the fullness of the means of salvation can be obtained" (Decree on Ecumenism, #3). Our duty then is to make these four marks visible in our daily lives so that others may see Jesus in us and want to follow Him.

The Virgin Mary

Everything that the Catholic Church teaches about Mary is based on what the Church teaches about Jesus. We revere Mary because she gave birth to Jesus, the Son of God and the second person of the Trinity. Catholics only worship God as a Trinity, but we revere Mary above all the Saints because of her special role in our Salvation. Jesus came to save us through Mary.

Mary is the Mother of God since she gave birth to Jesus who is the second person of the Trinity who is God. Jesus pre-existed Mary as the Word of God. The Word of God became Flesh through Mary. In Luke chapter 1, Elizabeth says "Why am I so favored, that the mother of my Lord should come to me?" Christians recognize that the "Lord" Elizabeth is referring to is Jesus, Jesus is God, Mary is the mother of Jesus, and therefore Mary is the mother of God. Jesus is fully God and fully man. Mary gave birth to God through the power of the Holy Spirit, the third person of the Trinity. If you separate Jesus' divine and human natures, than you separate the Trinity.

Mary was preserved from all sin by her Son Jesus before her birth to be a suitable Ark for the Word made Flesh.

The original Ark of the Old Testament was so Holy, no one could touch it. The original Ark held the Word of God in stone. Mary had the Word of God made Flesh in her womb, so it had to be at least as Holy as the first Ark. Mary was preserved, by Jesus, from original and personal sin so that she could bring us the sinless Messiah Jesus.

Mary is the Queen of Heaven because Jesus is the Messiah that would sit on the Throne of David. David's son Solomon had his mother as queen (1 Kings 2:19) and Solomon's family would ask his mother to ask Solomon for favors. In Revelation chapter 12 we find a woman in Heaven that gave birth to a man child who was to rule over the nations with a rod of iron. The predicted Messiah was to rule with a rod of iron. The Messiah is Jesus so the woman that bore Him who is in Heaven in Revelation chapter 12 must be Mary.

Mary is the New Eve because Paul calls Jesus the new "Adam" (1 Cor ch15). Jesus only refers to Mary as "Woman" in the New Testament (John ch2 and ch19) which tells us that she is the "woman" foretold in Genesis chapter2 who was to crush the head of the serpent (the devil). Mary defeats the devil by giving birth to Jesus who defeats Satan. Justin Martyr writes about Mary as the New Eve in 150AD and Irenaeus of Lyon wrote about Mary as the New Eve in 180AD. Justin and Irenaeus both learned about Christianity from the Apostle John's disciple Polycarp. So, this teaching comes from John through Polycarp to Justin and Irenaeus.

Mary is honored as the mother of ALL Christians because Jesus gave her to the beloved disciple John at the foot of the cross (John ch19). John is referred to as son, and as a representative of all Christians, took Mary into his home. In Revelation chapter 12 the dragon cannot get to Mary and Jesus, so he "went off to wage war against the rest of her offspring, those Christians who keep God's commands and hold fast their testimony about Jesus." All Christians try to keep God's commands; therefore, we can hold Mary as our spiritual mother through the Apostle John.

Mary is Ark of the New Covenant because Jesus is the Word made Flesh (John ch1) The original Ark of the Covenant held the Word on the tablets of stone and later the scrolls of the 5 books of Moses; Aaron's rod to symbolize authority and the miraculous Manna bread given to the Israelites in the desert. The end of Revelation chapter 11 has John looking into Heaven and he writes, "God's temple in heaven was opened, and within his temple was seen the Ark of His Covenant...a woman clothed with the sun". Mary is that Ark.
Compare these parallels between 2 Sam 6:5-11 (David with the Ark) and Luke 1:43,44 & 56 (Elizabeth with Mary).
1. David dances for joy in 2 Sam 6:5 and John leaps for joy in Elizabeth's womb in Luke 1:44. **2**. David calls out, "How can the ark of the Lord come to me?" in 2 Sam 6:9 and Elizabeth calls out, "why is this granted me, that the mother of my Lord should come to me?" in Luke 1:43.
3.The ark of the Lord remained in the house of Obed-Edom the Gittite a few miles outside Jerusalem for three months, and the Lord blessed Obed-Edom and his whole house in 2 Sam 6:11. Mary remained about three months with Elizabeth a few miles outside Jerusalem in Luke 1:56.

The perpetual virginity of Mary is easily shown in the Bible when Joseph and Mary lose Jesus when He stays behind in the Temple at Jerusalem. Joseph and Mary don't have any other children to worry about when Jesus is 12 years old (Luke ch2). At the foot of the cross (John ch19), Jesus gives Mary to John. In Jewish culture, the care of the mother passes to the eldest son after the father dies. Mary had no other sons, so Jesus gives Mary to John. In Luke chapter 1, engaged Mary asks HOW she will have a child, when the Angel Gabriel tells her she will have a child. Mary knew where babies came from but wasn't planning to have sex with a man. Mark chapter 6 lists James & Joses as brothers of Jesus, yet Matthew chapters 10and 27 tell us they have a different mother, Mary the wife of Cleopas. In Ezekiel 44:2, it says "The Lord said to me: This gate shall remain shut; it shall not be opened, and no one shall enter by it; for the Lord, the God of Israel, has entered by it; therefore, it shall remain shut." Mary is the gate through which Christ entered the world; no other person can enter that way. In Luke chapter 2 Jesus is called the firstborn, but this does not mean Mary had other children because 'first born' was a title for the Jews, denoting that son as the priest of the family. Luke 2:23, tells us "as it is written in the Law of the Lord, 'Every firstborn male is to be consecrated to the Lord" (Exodus ch13). The Jews did not have a word for cousin, so all close relatives were referred to as brothers and sisters. The Greek of the original New Testament has a word for cousin but the words for brother and sister are used with the original Jewish understanding.

Mary was assumed into Heaven, so she could be the Queen of the new Messiah, Jesus, in Heaven. Enoch & Elijah are assumed bodily into Heaven (Genesis 5:24, 2 Kings 2, 1 Macc 2:58, Sirach 44:16 and 49:14, Heb 11:5) so Jesus could do the same for His Mother. The assumption of Mary is an Apostolic Tradition held by Catholic and Orthodox Christians. The history of the Assumption of Mary is recorded as early as 180AD when Melito of Sardis wrote a corrective letter about an earlier account of the Assumption of Mary. In 451AD, at the Council of Chalcedon, were the two Consubstantial Natures of Christ were declared Dogma, the Roman emperor asked for a relic of Mary to add to his collection of Apostle and Saint relics. St. Juvenal explained to the emperor that we have no True Relics of Mary because she was assumed into Heaven.

Mary is an intercessor for Christians because she is the Queen mother of the Messiah Jesus. Mary first intercedes for us with Jesus in John chapter 2 when she tells Jesus they have run out of wine at the wedding at Cana. Jesus provides more wine through a miracle through the intercession of Mary.

The 'Hail Mary' is from the Bible: Hail, Full of Grace, the Lord is with you" (Luke 1:28)"Blessed are you among women and Blessed is the fruit of your womb" (Luke 1:42). Hail Mary, "Mother of God" (Luke1:43 Elizabeth calls Mary this). Pray for us, now and at the hour of our death like she did at Jesus death John 19:25 The Church honors Mary this way to fulfill God's promise to her in Luke 1:48 "All generations shall call me blessed"

The rosary is a Bible study on a chain of beads guiding us to think about 20 events in the life of Jesus. The prayers come from the Bible: "Our Father"; (Matt 6:9-13). "Hail Mary"; (Luke ch1, John ch19). The Rosary is our weapon against Satan. Like David's sling, with which he defeated Goliath (1 Sam 17:40). The 5 decades are like the 5 stones David took from the stream.

Jesus death on the cross and His later resurrection provides sufficient Grace for our Salvation. Mary provided us with Jesus through God's plan for our Salvation. Mary is a co-mediator in our salvation because she gave birth to Jesus the true Mediator for our Salvation. Just as we can ask people on earth to pray to God for us, we can also ask Mary to pray to Jesus for us. As the Queen Mother she is close to her Son the King Jesus Christ.

Praying with Mary, the Angels and Saints

Catholics pray with Mary and the Saints, but Protestants don't because they say the Bible teaches against this practice. In 1st Timothy 2:5 Paul says there is only one mediator between God and man, the man Jesus Christ. Also, Jesus said in John 14:13-14, "And I will do whatever you ask in my name, so that the Father may be glorified in the Son. You may ask me for anything in my NAME and I will do it"

Protestants have been taught that praying to Mary and the Saints takes away from God's Glory or is forbidden in the book of Deuteronomy chapter 18. This is because their theology tells them that they are hidden in Christ when they come to believe in Him, so they are not actually members of the Body of Christ.

Catholics also recognize Jesus as the sole Mediator between God and man. Catholics also recognize that we are members of the Body of Christ through Baptism (1 Cor ch12). In 1 Tim 1:2, Paul writes "First of all, then, I urge that supplications, prayers, intercessions, and thanksgivings be made for all men," So we are expected to intercede for each other. To strictly follow 1 Timothy 2:5 where Jesus is the sole Mediator, is to disallow the prayers of friends and family on earth because it makes them a mediator between God and man. Paul does not teach us to pray for one another in the first chapter and to *not* pray for one another in the second chapter. Paul is teaching that we can all pray to the one Mediator Jesus as members of the same Body of Christ. In 1st Corinthians chapter 3 Paul tells us we are co-laborers with Christ. In James chapter 5 we learn that the prayers of the righteous are powerful, so it is logical to ask those in Heaven and closest to Jesus to pray for us too. In Matthew chapter 22 and Mark chapter 12, Jesus said He is the God of Abraham, and the God of Isaac, and the God of Jacob. God is not the God of the dead, but of the living. This shows the Old Testament Saints are alive in Heaven. In Revelation chapters 5 and 8 the prayers of the Saints are shown to be offered in Heaven. Our prayers to Mary and the Saints are the ones offered in Jesus's name, to God, in Heaven.

Mary has a special role as the Queen of Heaven. To understand why she is the Queen of Heaven first we must understand the role of the Queen Mother in the Old Testament. In 1st Kings Chapter 2 we find the story of King Solomon. Solomon was the first King to sit on the Throne of David. Solomon had 700 wives and 300 concubines, so he chose his mother to be Queen in his court. Solomon's own siblings appealed to him through the intersession of the Queen Mother Bathsheba. This tradition was carried on by all the Kings of Israel afterward until the Babylonians conquered all of Israel. The coming Messiah was prophesied to sit on the Throne of David. Jesus is the Messiah that sits on the Throne of David in the Heavenly Jerusalem. Mary is His Queen Mother that offers our intersessions to her Son in Heaven. In the epilogue of the book Heaven is for Real, Colton said he saw Mary praying before Jesus. This confirms the Catholic teaching because Colton is the son of a Wesleyan minister and was not brought up to think of Mary having any special role. In Revelation chapter 12 we find the Ark of the Covenant in Heaven clothed with the sun, crowned with stars and the moon at her feet. This woman gives birth to the Man Child that will rule with a rod of iron. We understand Jesus to be that Man Child and only one woman gave birth to Him. That woman is Mary. Mary is the New Eve, born of nation of Israel, without sin and preserved from sin so her womb could be the Ark of the New Covenant holding the Word made Flesh, Jesus Christ. Mary is the woman that John saw in Heaven who can offer our prayers to her Son, Jesus.

As Catholics we understand that we are made members of the Body of Christ through Baptism (1 Cor ch12). Just as we ask friends and family here on earth to ask Jesus for help, we can ask Mary and the Saints to ask Jesus for help. Any help we receive comes from Jesus. Mary and the Saints have no abilities on their own to grant favors. They can only ask God on our behalf like our friends and family on earth. Jesus is the Head of the Body of Christ that all Christians are members of. One part of the body communicates to the other parts of the body through the Head which is Jesus Christ. In 1 Corinthians chapter 6, Paul tells Christians not to unite the Body of Christ to a prostitute, so we know that we are a part of the Body of Christ, not "hidden" in Christ.

The Angels are spiritual beings. Humans are Physical and Spiritual beings. The Saints are holy ones in Heaven. A category open to both beings created by God. We ask St. Michael the Archangel to pray for us because he intercedes for us in his constant battle against Satan to restrain his activity. Humans can be declared Saints when there is sufficient evidence that they are in Heaven and pray for us directly to God. We are all called to become saints (note small s) in our life here on earth. As members of the Body of Christ, His Church, we can all help each other. The Church consists of the Church Triumphant in Heaven; the Church Suffering in Purgatory; and the Church Militant here on earth. These three groups make up the Communion of Saints.

Early References of praying with Mary and the Saints:
Shepherd of Hermas 100AD,
 Clement of Alexandria 208AD,
Hippolytus of Rome 215AD,
Origen of Alexandria 233AD. Hymn to Father, Son and Holy Spirit may all the powers (Saints) join in with us to say Amen.
Prayer to Theotokos (Mary) on Egyptian papyrus 250AD.
Methodius prayer to Mary 305AD,
There are inscriptions on tombs asking deceased Christians to pray for the living 300-325AD.
St. Cyprian of Carthage 253AD writes about Christians praying with the Saints as well as Cyril of Jerusalem 350AD, Hilary of Poitiers 365AD, Ephraim the Syrian 370AD, The Liturgy of St. Basil 373AD, Pectorius 375AD, Gregory of Nazianz 380 AD, Gregory of Nyssa 380AD, John Chrysostom 392AD,
Ambrose of Milan 393AD
All write about praying through and with the Saints.

Statues, Images and Relics in Church

Catholic Christians and Protestant Christians both agree that the Ten Commandments forbid the making of images for worship (Exodus ch20). After God gave this commandment, He ordered Moses to build an Ark with two great big statues on it (Exodus ch25, 26&30). The Israelites understood that the space between the wings of the two Cherubim was the Mercy Seat of God. God also commands Moses to build a portable Temple that has images woven into fabric to adorn the Temple (Exodus ch36). This shows that God does not forbid statues or religious images just the worship of them.

Later God commands Moses to make a staff with a bronze statue of a serpent on it (Num ch21). When the Israelites look upon this statue, they are healed of their snake bites. Later when the Israelites start to worship the bronze statue of the serpent, God orders that the statue be destroyed. This shows that statues can be a source of healing but can also be abused.

Solomon later builds the Temple specified by God to David (1 Kings ch6). This temple had two 30-foot-tall statues in front by the entrance. This same Temple had statues inside and images woven into fabric hangings. Again, God does not have a problem with statues and images in His worship space. The Temple is also adorned with gold, silver and precious wood because it is appropriate for us to use our best gifts from God in our worship of God.

In 2 Kings chapter 13 we have the story of a dead Israelite soldier that is hastily thrown into Elisha's tomb and is brought back to life by touching Elisha's bones. This is an early demonstration that God's Grace and healing can be transferred to another person by touching a part of a Holy dead person.

The Jews at the time of Christ, and the early Christians most of whom were Jews, were used to using statues and images as part of their worship. Early Churches and Synagogues of the same time had images painted on the walls to show the teachings of Scripture because most people couldn't read and couldn't afford their own copy of Scripture.

Paul writes in Galatians 3:1, "O foolish Galatians! Who has bewitched you, before whose eyes Jesus Christ was publicly portrayed as crucified?" Jesus was publicly portrayed, before their **eyes**, as being crucified. This sounds like they were looking at a Crucifix. Galatia is far from Jerusalem where Jesus was crucified. Few if any of the Galatians mentioned here would have been at Jesus crucifixion.

In the Book of Acts chapter 5 we find that people were brought out to be laid along the path that Peter would take on his way to the Temple so that his shadow might fall upon them and these people were healed. This shows that God's Grace and healing can be transmitted to others merely by being close to a holy person. In Acts chapter 19 we find that handkerchiefs and aprons touched to the Apostles could heal other people. These are what the Catholic Church now calls 2nd class relics. They are physical things that bring God's Grace and healing to others. Blessed oil and Holy water are also physical things that can bring God's healing and Grace to someone who is open to that Grace and if it is part of God's plan that they should be healed.

The first Churches built by the early Christians were built over the tombs of the first martyrs so that they could be close to the holy relics of the early Christians. When Ignatius of Antioch was eaten by lions his leftover bones were saved as relics in 107AD. When Polycarp Bishop of Smyrna was burned at the stake his bones were also saved as relics around 155AD. This shows that from the beginning the early Christians recognized that the holiness of the Saints and Martyrs continued in their relics after they died. It was the pagans that thought saving the bones of dead people was bad.

The Second Council of Nicaea in 787AD declared that Churches are allowed to have images to help in the worship of God. This Council was guided by the Holy Spirit like the first Ecumenical Council of Jerusalem in Acts chapter 15. This Council had the authority to bind and loose given through Apostolic Succession by Jesus from Matthew's Gospel chapters 16 and 28.

Until the late 1400s all books had to be copied by hand. The invention of movable type allowed for the mass production of books. The first book copied with the new moveable type was the Bible that still consisted of 2 large volumes. This improved way of copying the Bible still took several months to print but that was better than the 1 or 2 years it took to copy it by hand.

For three quarters of the history of Christianity, the Faith was passed on through statues, images and preaching, not a book. The stained-glass windows of the Churches built in the Middle Ages told the stories of Jesus in their images and were accessible to anyone who could see them. When the new Protestant denominations were started by the man that founded them in the early 1500s, they had access to cheap copies of the Bible with which to share the Word of God. Protestants have always had cheap access to the Bible that the Catholic Church preserved for 1500 years by copying it by hand.

The Catholic and Orthodox Churches continue to use statues and images as Holy reminders of our Christian heritage. We have no images of God but recognize His presence in the Tabernacle that contains the Eucharist.

The real presence of Jesus in the Tabernacle is the only thing we bow to. We have statues of Mary and the Saints to remind us to follow their example in leading a good Christian life. Catholic Churches have images on the Stations of the Cross which tell the story of Jesus passion, death and resurrection for our salvation. These images are still available to anyone who can see, and they still teach the Gospel of Jesus death and resurrection for our salvation. Many Catholic Churches have stained glass windows that show other stories from the life of Jesus and His Church.

All of this easy to understand sharing of the good news of Jesus death and resurrection for our salvation is available for free to anyone to see. People interested in Christianity don't have to buy a Bible to learn about it. All they have to do is go to a Catholic Church that is open every day. They can hear the Old and New Testament read to them for free every day at the Catholic Church. The Catholic Church provides a free explanation of the Bible readings in the Homily every day for those who are new to Christianity.

The relics of the Saints remind us of the holy heroes that have gone before us. Statues and images do the same thing. There is no need to be afraid of statues and images in Churches as long as you remember their true function is to remind us of Jesus sacrifice for us and that we worship God alone. Anything granted to us through the intersession of Mary and the Saints comes to us through the power of Jesus.

In the late 300sAD St. Jerome, who did the official Latin Translation of the Bible known as the Vulgate wrote, "We do not WORSHIP the relics of the Martyrs, we HONOR them in our WORSHIP of JESUS whose Martyrs they are. We honor the servants in order that the respect paid to them can be REFLECTED BACK TO JESUS."

The Truth About the Rapture

Many Christians believe in the Rapture. Some believe the Bible says there will be a Pre-Tribulation Rapture. Some say the Bible says there will be a Mid –Tribulation Rapture. Some say the Bible says there will be a Post-Tribulation Rapture. Some say there will be all three. All these interpretations come from some verses in the Bible and some persons understanding of them.

But some churches don't teach the doctrine of the Rapture. All of the churches started before 1800 don't teach the doctrine of the Rapture. These Churches include the Catholic Church, the Orthodox Church, the Lutheran, Reformed and Presbyterian Churches, the Anglican, Episcopal, Methodist and Wesleyan Churches, the Quakers, the Church of Christ and the Amish.

This is because the Rapture was invented in the 1830s by a man named John Nelson Darby. His interpretation of the Bible was promoted through the Scofield Study Bible that is used in a lot of Protestant Seminaries. John Walvoord is considered the Dean of the Pre-tribulation Rapture at Dallas Theological Seminary. He wrote a book called "The Rapture Question". In his book he writes: "The early Church did not teach 20th century pre-tribulationism." 'The early church teaching can only be described as post tribulational.' 'The Early Church Fathers were post tribulational'.

Matthew chapter 24 tells the story of the "one is taken, one is left" passage. In this chapter we learn that After the Tribulation the coming of the Son of Man will be accompanied by the earth shaking, and the sun and moon will be darkened. The bad people are taken away and the good people are left behind in the ark that Noah built. However, you could say Noah's family was taken away in the ark and the bad people were left behind to drown in the flood. The story is repeated in Luke's Gospel with more clarity.

If you read all of Luke chapter 17 you will get the whole story of the "one is taken, and one is left". The coming of the Son of Man will be accompanied by lightning flashes, thunder, and earth shaking. It will be like the days of Noah and Lot where the bad people were who are taken away in the flood or the destruction of Sodom and the good people were left behind in the ark or as Lot and his family. It also provides clarification where the people taken away go to. In verse 37 it says the bad people who are taken go to where the vultures gather. The place where vultures gather is for dead people, not Heaven.

If you read all of 1 Thessalonians chapter 4 you will get the whole story here too. Paul tells us in the beginning that when Jesus comes back there will be trumpets sounding and the dead will rise first. It does not say that there will be a secret disappearing of believers, with the dead will still in the ground which is the typical teaching of the rapture. Chapter 4 says that the dead and believers will be caught up in the air to meet Him, but it doesn't say they will return to Heaven. Those that are caught up (raptured) will accompany Jesus on His way down to earth to set up His new Kingdom. This is another example of Jesus' second coming like in Matthew chapter 24, Luke chapter 17, 1 Corinthians chapter 15 and John chapter 6. Rapture believers like to skip the early verses that describe the second coming and quote verses 13 to18, "We do not want you to be unaware, brothers, about those who have fallen asleep, so that you may not grieve like the rest, who have no hope. For if we believe that Jesus died and rose, so too will God, through Jesus, bring with him those who have fallen asleep. Indeed, we tell you this, on the word of the Lord, that we who are alive, who are left until the coming of the Lord, will surely not precede those who have fallen asleep. For the Lord himself, with a word of command, with the voice of an archangel and with the trumpet of God, will come down from heaven, and the dead in Christ will rise first. Then we who are alive, who are left, will be caught up together with them in the clouds to meet the Lord in the air. Thus, we shall always be with the Lord. Therefore, console one another with these words." There is no verse that says Jesus returns to Heaven after dead and living are caught up.

The Bible says we are not appointed to wrath, but it doesn't say we are not appointed to tribulation. Wrath is punishment by God. Tribulation is testing by God. In 1 Thessalonians chapter 3 Paul says we have to endure tribulation. In John chapter 16:33 it says, "I have said this to you, that in me you may have peace. In the world you will have tribulation; but be of good cheer, I have overcome the world." In Matthew chapter 24, it says we will have to endure the "Great Tribulation" before he writes the passages about "one being taken and one left" In Acts 14:22 it says "...strengthening the souls of the disciples, exhorting them to continue in the faith, and saying that through many tribulations we must enter the kingdom of God."

In Revelation chapter 1 it says that when Jesus comes back, He will be coming in the clouds and every eye will see Him including those who pierced Him. All believers and non-believers will see Jesus when He returns. Only those that are fully Holy will enter Heaven according to Revelation chapter 21.

If you read all of John chapter 6, John tells us Jesus will raise us on the Last Day. The Final Judgement at the Last Day is described in chapter 12. The Bible says Jesus is only coming back once, on the Last Day, not one and a half times. If you read all of the Bible it is hard to believe in the Rapture.

A Catholic view on the End Times.

We should always live our life with the expectation that Jesus is coming back today. This is why we always need to keep ourselves in a State of Grace.

One of the signs of Jesus' return is the rise of the Anti-Christ. There will be a large percentage of the Jews that will turn to Jesus and become Christians or fulfilled Jews. Those anticipating Jesus return may be caught up to meet Him as He returns to earth to set up His Kingdom here on earth. The dead will get their resurrected and perfected bodies back. The living will receive perfected immortal bodies.

Then there will be the Final Judgement where all our past deeds will be revealed and how they effected the rest of the world. We will see God's justice for those that are headed to Hell for eternal punishment. We will also see how our good deeds affected others and how many times God has forgiven us for our sins. Everyone that will be living in the new Heaven on earth will be fully filled with Grace, but some will have a greater capacity to be filled with Grace based on their deeds in this life.

The Catechism of the Catholic Church covers the End Times in paragraphs 668-682; 1021; and 1038-1041.

When you look at the Book of Revelation as it relates to the Mass, you see the reading of the letters in the first 4 chapters. This corresponds to the Liturgy of the Word (4 Bible readings) in the Mass. Then John is caught up to Heaven for the Heavenly Eucharistic Liturgy. This is the Wedding Supper of the Lamb where Jesus and His Church bride are permanently united.

How to use this information for Evangelization

You: What church do you attend? **OR** Which faith tradition do you follow?

Friend: I attend *Ken Bob's First Baptist, New Testament, Full Gospel, Bible church.*

You: Have you ever wondered what Christians were doing before they had a Bible?

Friend: What do mean? We have always had a Bible.

You: The Catholic Church did not establish which early Christian writings would make up the Bible until 382AD at the earliest. If you would like to learn a little about

what Christians were doing before they had a Bible, read
Justin Martyr's First Apology on Christianity to the
Roman Emperor Antoninus written in 150AD.
**Additional Resources: Apologists, Books and
Websites**
Why We're Catholic by Trent Horn
The Case for Catholicism by Trent Horn
Answering Atheism by Trent Horn
Nuts and Bolts by Tim Staples
Behold Your Mother by Tim Staples
A Daily Defense by Jimmy Akin
The Drama of Salvation by Jimmy Akin
Mass Confusion by Jimmy Akin
The Fathers Know Best by Jimmy Akin
Crossing the Tiber by Steve Ray
Upon This Rock by Steve Ray
Reasons to Believe by Scott Hahn
A Father Who Keeps His Promises by Scott Hahn
Evangelizing Catholics by Scott Hahn
Hail Holy Queen by Scott Hahn
Catholicism and Fundamentalism by Karl Keating
What Catholics Really Believe by Karl Keating
From Synagogue to Church by James Tunstead Burchill
The Seven Deadly Sins of Apologetics by Mark Brumley
How Not to Share Your Faith by Mark Brumley
One Minute Apologist by Dave Armstrong
Proving the Catholic Faith is Biblical by Dave Armstrong
Search and Rescue by Patrick Madrid
How to Do Apologetics by Patrick Madrid
A Pocket Guide to Catholic Apologetics by Patrick Madrid
Handbook of Apologetics by Peter Kreeft + Ronald Tacelli
Fundamentals of the Faith by Peter Kreeft
Why Catholic Bibles Are Bigger by Gary Michuta
Hostile Witness by Gary Michuta
The Protestants Dilemma by Devin Rose
Navigating the Tiber by Devin Rose

How to Share Your Faith with Anyone by Terry Barber
Dangers to the Faith by Al Kresta
Handed Down Faith of the Early Christians by Jim
Papandrea
How to Explain and Defend the Catholic Faith by Fr.
Frank Chacon and Jim Burnham
Faith of the Early Church by Fr. Nicholas Gregoris
Why Do Catholics Do That? by Kevin Orlin Johnson
Beginning Apologetic Series from Catholic Answers
The Essential Catholic Survival Guide by Various Catholic
Answers Authors
95 Questions for Protestants by Roger & Karen Salstrom
Confessions of a Street Evangelist by Frederick Marks
8 Essential Truths that Every Catholic Should Know by
John LaBarbara
How to Win Friends to Christ by Fr. Thomas Cavanaugh

Websites
Catholic Answers Frequently Asked Questions
EWTN Frequently Asked Questions
New Advent and Early Christian Writings
USCCB.org and Vatican.org
John Martignoni Bible Christian Society and Facebook
page

About the Author

As a cradle Catholic, I grew up in the Catholic Church and went through the sacrament assembly line. I followed the Faith out of habit.

In 2005 I started taking the Faith more seriously. It was a slow but steady deepening in the Faith.

In 2010, I read the Left Behind books which started my investigation into the rapture. Scott Hahn and Tim Staples saved me from falling into the "rapture trap" and inspired me to go deeper into the Catholic Faith. This led me to other Catholic Apologists and the writings of the Early Church Fathers. They inspired me to do my own research and study of the Bible. I now have more than 10,000 hours of research into a variety of related topics, from ancient civilizations to the Bible as we have it today.

In 2015, I came to the realization that I have an obligation to share the Truth I have learned with my fellow Catholics and non-Catholics. The Catholic Church is the only complete Church that goes all the way back to the beginning of Christianity.

If you have any questions or comments or would like me to speak to your group, I can be contacted at kenlitchfield61@gmail.com or on Facebook.

I also have many videos and playlists on my YouTube channel that can help you learn more about the Catholic Faith.

Made in the USA
Middletown, DE
17 March 2019